VEGETARIAN MICROWAVE RECIPES

VEGETARIAN MICROWAVE RECIPES

Sue Locke

W. Foulsham & Co. Ltd.

London • New York • Toronto • Cape Town • Sydney

W. Foulsham & Company Limited
Yeovil Road, Slough, Berkshire, SL1 4JH

ISBN 0-572-01393-0

Printed in Spain by Cayfosa, Barcelona.
Dep. Leg. B- 32320-1986

CONTENTS

INTRODUCTION

The microwave oven is one of the most exciting developments to come into the kitchen this century. For me, it is an essential part of living and working in the 'eighties'. There are many advantages apart from the obvious such as timesaving, laboursaving and the low running cost. I hope you will discover for yourself some of these advantages with the help of this new book.

I was particularly pleased to be asked to write this book as it is absolutely my style of living and eating. The microwave oven is particularly appropriate for cooking vegetables as they retain all their natural flavour, colour and vitamins. If cooked carefully, they are wonderfully crunchy and, in some cases, taste quite different.

This book should inspire those of you who have been considering becoming vegetarian and, similarly, long established vegetarians. It should also be useful for those on low fat diets and for those who have decided, for various reasons, to reduce their meat intake.

There are a number of things to be aware of when making your first steps towards vegetarianism. Always be sure to have lots of variety; there is so much to choose from so try to have one meal a day which is raw vegetables and salad with, perhaps, one of the dishes in this book. The important thing is to be sure to have adequate protein every day. The body needs protein. It is essential for building and protecting body cells. It is a continual process and it is important to maintain the very particular balance required for good health.

Protein is found in many foods besides meat and fish. Important sources of protein for vegetarians are eggs, cheese, dairy products, nuts, vegetables and, in particular, pulse foods such as lentils, beans, split peas, chick peas, etc. Ideally, your daily protein should be taken from at least three of these sources. This will ensure the correct supply of amino acids required for body growth and protection, in short, *good health*.

The recipes in this book were created and tested with the help of the Brother Hi-Speed cooker which has the added advantage of having a microwave setting, a turbo setting and a hi-speed setting for browning food which is the only disadvantage with some microwave cookers. When choosing a microwave try, if possible, to get the oven demonstrated in the store and get the best you can afford, preferably with a turntable and a browning facility. I hope you enjoy experimenting with this book and your microwave.

Important Tips when Using a Microwave

Always make sure there is something inside the oven if it is on. Be especially careful if a time-setting is on and you have removed the dish.

Allow food to rest a minute or two after removing from the oven to complete cooking.

Always wipe oven clean after use. Debris in the oven attracts the microwaves.

Use oven gloves or a cloth to remove dishes from the oven as they can be hot.

Prick any food with a skin such as potatoes, tomatoes and apples otherwise they will burst.

Do not boil eggs in a microwave as they will burst. Prick egg yolks when using whole eggs.

The effect of steaming food can be achieved by covering dish with a lid or plate, leaving a gap to allow steam to escape. Use microwave roast-bags whenever appropriate. Use medium setting whenever appropriate. This is often neglected.

Use low setting for defrosting.

Do not overcook food.

Always use appropriate microwave utensils.

Do not use metal or tin containers in microwaves.

At the present time, there is some doubt about the use of cling film in the microwave. It is thought by some to be a health hazard.

Microwave Magic

Reheat cold coffee	Microwave HIGH 2 mins
Freshen stale coffee beans	Microwave HIGH 2 mins
Soften jelly	Microwave HIGH 1 min
Soften ice-cream	Microwave HIGH 1 min
Soften sorbet ice-cream	Microwave HIGH 30 secs
Soften butter	Microwave HIGH 30 secs
Soften marzipan	Microwave HIGH 15 secs
Roast nuts	Microwave HIGH 3 mins
To get more juice from lemons and oranges	Microwave HIGH 30 secs
Soften Brie cheese	Microwave HIGH 30 secs
Dry fresh herbs	Microwave HIGH 30 secs
Soften honey	Microwave HIGH 1 min
Soften butter and sugar for creaming	Microwave HIGH 20 secs
Peel tomatoes – prick and place in water	Microwave HIGH 30 secs
Skin almonds	Microwave HIGH 1 min
Soften old brown sugar	Microwave HIGH 1 min

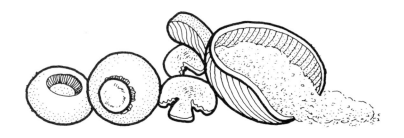

Timings Conversion Table

Please note that all the timings in this book are based on a 600 watt microwave oven. If you have a 500 watt or 700 watt oven you can convert the timings easily using this chart. All timings are approximate – and remember, it is better to undercook than overcook as dishes can always be returned to the microwave for a few more seconds.

500 watt	600 watt	650 700 watt
45s	30s	3 7 15s
1m 25s	1m	35s
2m 50s	2m	1m 15s
4m 15s	3m	1m 45s
5m 40s	4m	2m 20s
7m	5m	3m
8m 30s	6m	3m 30s
10m	7m	4m
11m 20s	8m	4m 40s
12m 45s	9m	5m 15s
14m	10m	6m
15m 35s	11m	6m 40s
17m	12m	7m
18m 25s	13m	7m 35s
19m 50s	14m	8m
21m 15s	15m	8m 45s
22m 40s	16m	9m 15s
24m	17m	9m 50s
25m 30s	18m	10m 30s
27m	19m	11m
28m 20s	20m	11m 40s
29m 45s	21m	12m 15s
32m 35s	22m	12m 45s
34m	23m	13m 20s
35m 25s	24m	14m
35m 50s	25m	14m 35s
37m 15s	26m	15m
38m 40s	27m	15m 35s
40m	28m	16m 15s
41m 25s	29md	6m 45s
42m 50s	30m	17m 20s

1 SOUPS

Parsnip and Peanut Soup

Serves 6

INGREDIENTS	Imperial	Metric	American
Onion	2 medium	2 medium	2 medium
Garlic	2 cloves	2 cloves	2 cloves
Vegetable oil	2 tbsp	2 tbsp	2 tbsp
Parsnip	12 oz	350 g	12 oz
Vegetable stock	1 pt	575 ml	2 1/2 cups
Peanut butter	2 tbsp	2 tbsp	2 tbsp
Sea salt	1 tsp	1 tsp	1 tsp
Freshly ground black pepper			
Mixed spice	1/2 tsp	1/2 tsp	1/2 tsp
Single cream	2 tbsp	2 tbsp	2 tbsp
GARNISH			
Chopped parsley			

1. Chop the onion and the garlic and place in a glass bowl with the vegetable oil. Microwave HIGH for 3 minutes.

2. Peel and slice the parsnips and make the vegetable stock. Add to the onion and garlic along with the peanut butter and seasonings. Cover with a lid or plate, leaving a gap to allow steam to escape. Microwave HIGH for 10 minutes.

3. Process for 1 minute in a food processor or sieve. Stir in the single cream and garnish with chopped parsley.

Winter Vegetable Soup

Serves 8

INGREDIENTS	Imperial	Metric	American
Onion	*1 medium*	*1 medium*	*1 medium*
Garlic	*2 cloves*	*2 cloves*	*2 cloves*
Celery	*2 sticks*	*2 sticks*	*2 sticks*
Vegetable oil	*2 tbsp*	*2 tbsp*	*2 tbsp*
Potato	*1 large*	*1 large*	*1 large*
Carrots	*2 medium*	*2 medium*	*2 medium*
Parsnips	*2 medium*	*2 medium*	*2 medium*
Turnip	*1 small*	*1 small*	*1 small*
Courgettes	*2 medium*	*2 medium*	*2 medium*
Vegetable stock	*1 pt*	*600 ml*	*2 ½ cups*
Sea salt	*1 tsp*	*1 tsp*	*1 tsp*
Freshly ground black pepper			
Mixed herbs	*1 tsp*	*1 tsp*	*1 tsp*

1. Slice and chop the onion, garlic and celery and place in a glass bowl. Pour on the vegetable oil. Microwave HIGH for 3 minutes.

2. Dice the potato, carrots, parsnips and turnip. Slice the courgettes. Place all the vegetables in a glass bowl along with the vegetable stock and seasoning.

3. Cover with a lid or plate, leaving a gap to allow steam to escape. Microwave HIGH for 10 minutes. Stir once in cooking process. Delicious served very hot with crunchy wholemeal bread and butter.

Green Pea and Nutmeg Soup

Serves 6

INGREDIENTS	Imperial	Metric	American
Lettuce heart	1 small	1 small	1 small
Onion	1 medium	1 medium	1 medium
Garlic	2 cloves	2 cloves	2 cloves
Celery	1 stick	1 stick	1 stick
Vegetable oil	2 tbsp	2 tbsp	2 tbsp
Frozen peas	12 oz	350 g	12 oz
Vegetable stock	1 pt	600 ml	2½ cups
Sea salt	1 tsp	1 tsp	1 tsp
Freshly ground black pepper			
Nutmeg	½ tsp	½ tsp	½ tsp
Single cream	2 tbsp	2 tbsp	2 tbsp
GARNISH			
Freshly chopped mint			

1. Slice and chop the lettuce heart, onion, garlic and celery stick and place in a glass bowl. Pour on the vegetable oil. Microwave HIGH for 3 minutes.

2. Combine the peas and the vegetable stock and place with the seasonings in the glass bowl along with the other vegetables. Cover with a lid or plate, leaving a gap to allow steam to escape. Microwave HIGH for 8 minutes. Stir once in cooking.

3. Process for 1 minute in a food processor or sieve. Add the cream and process again. Serve garnished with chopped mint.

Chinese Vegetable Soup

Serves 8

INGREDIENTS	Imperial	Metric	American
Onion	1 medium	1 medium	1 medium
Garlic	2 cloves	2 cloves	2 cloves
Root ginger	1/2 in	1.5 cm	1/2 in
Cardamon seeds	6	6	6
Vegetable oil	2 tbsp	2 tbsp	2 tbsp
Red pepper	1 medium	1 medium	1 medium
Mange tout	12	12	12
Mung sprouts	2 tbsp	2 tbsp	2 tbsp
Chinese cabbage	4 oz	100 g	4 oz
Bean sprouts	2 oz	50 g	2 oz
Vegetable stock	1 pt	600 ml	1 pt
Sea salt	1 tsp	1 tsp	1 tsp
Freshly ground black pepper			
Chinese 5 spice	1/2 tsp	1/2 tsp	1/2 tsp

1. Chop the onion, garlic and ginger root very fine and place in a glass bowl with the cardamon seeds. Add the oil and microwave HIGH for 3 minutes.

2. Prepare the remaining vegetables. Top and tail the mange tout. Slice the red pepper and the cabbage. (Ordinary cabbage will do if Chinese cabbage is not available.) Add all the remaining ingredients to the glass bowl.

3. Cover with a lid or plate, leaving a gap to allow steam to escape. Microwave HIGH for 8 minutes so that vegetables are still crisp. Stir once during cooking process.

Carrot, Potato and Onion Soup

Serves 8

INGREDIENTS	Imperial	Metric	American
Onions	2 medium	2 medium	2 medium
Garlic	2 cloves	2 cloves	2 cloves
Vegetable oil	2 tbsp	2 tbsp	2 tbsp
Carrot	4 medium	4 medium	4 medium
Potato	1 large	1 large	1 large
Vegetable stock	1 pt	600 ml	1 pt
Sea salt	1 tsp	1 tsp	1 tsp
Freshly ground black pepper			
Curry powder	1 tsp	1 tsp	1 tsp
Single cream	5 oz	135 g	5 oz
Milk	1/4 pt	225 ml	1/4 pt
GARNISH			
Croutons	2 tbsp	2 tbsp	2 tbsp

1. Slice the onions and garlic. Place with vegetable oil in a glass bowl and microwave HIGH for 3 minutes.

2. Prepare the carrots and potato by peeling and dicing them. Add, with the vegetable stock, to the onion mixture. Add seasoning. Stir well and cover with a lid or plate, leaving a gap to allow steam to escape. Microwave HIGH for 12 minutes. Remove and process in a food processor for 2 minutes or sieve. Add the cream and milk. Process again.

3. Return the mixture to a glass bowl and microwave HIGH for 3 minutes. Serve with croutons.

Leek and Artichoke Soup

Serves 6

INGREDIENTS	Imperial	Metric	American
Leek	1 medium	1 medium	1 medium
Garlic	2 cloves	2 cloves	2 cloves
Carrots	2 medium	2 medium	2 medium
Vegetable oil	2 tbsp	2 tbsp	2 tbsp
Jerusalem artichoke, peeled	12 oz	350 g	12 oz
Vegetable stock	1 pt	600 ml	2½ cups
Sea Salt	1 tsp	1 tsp	1 tsp
Freshly ground black pepper			
Caraway seeds	½ tsp	½ tsp	½ tsp
Double cream	5 oz	135 g	5 oz
Milk	¼ pt	225 ml	¾ cup

GARNISH
Sunflower seeds

1. Slice the leek, garlic and carrots and place in a glass bowl. Add the vegetable oil and microwave HIGH for 3 minutes.

2. Add the chopped artichoke and vegetable stock. Add the seasoning. Cover with a lid or plate, leaving a gap to allow steam to escape. Microwave HIGH for 12 minutes.

3. Remove and process in a food processor for 2 minutes or in a sieve. Add the double cream and milk and process again.

4. Place in a glass bowl again and cover as before. Microwave MEDIUM for 3 minutes. Garnish with sunflower seeds.

Tomato and Orange Soup

Serves 8

INGREDIENTS	Imperial	Metric	American
Onion	1 medium	1 medium	1 medium
Garlic	2 cloves	2 cloves	2 cloves
Vegetable oil	2 tbsp	2 tbsp	2 tbsp
Tomatoes	6 large	6 large	6 large
Vegetable stock	1 pt	600 ml	1 pt
Tomato purée	2 tbsp	2 tbsp	2 tbsp
Orange, juice and rind	1 large	1 large	1 large
Sea salt	1 tsp	1 tsp	1 tsp
Freshly ground black pepper			
Fresh basil	1 tbsp	1 tbsp	1 tbsp
Brown sugar	1 tsp	1 tsp	1 tsp

GARNISH
Croutons

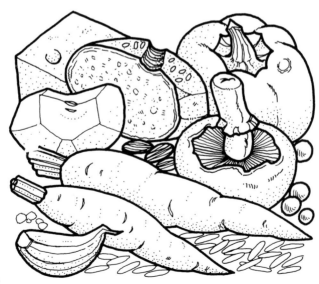

1. Chop the onion and the garlic. Place in a glass bowl with the vegetable oil. Microwave HIGH for 3 minutes.

2. Skin the tomatoes and chop. Add to the vegetable stock together with the tomato purée, orange rind and juice and seasoning. Add to the glass bowl and cover with a lid or plate, leaving a gap to allow steam to escape. Microwave HIGH for 10 minutes. Stir once during the cooking process.

3. Remove and place in a food processor and process for 2 minutes or sieve the mixture. Serve with croûtons.

Cream of Mushroom Soup

Serves 8

INGREDIENTS	Imperial	Metric	American
Onion	1 medium	1 medium	1 medium
Garlic	2 cloves	2 cloves	2 cloves
Celery	1 stick	1 stick	1 stick
Vegetable oil	2 tbsp	2 tbsp	2 tbsp
Flat field mushrooms	12 oz	350 g	12 oz
Vegetable stock	1 pt	600 ml	1 pt
Sea salt	1 tsp	1 tsp	1 tsp
Freshly ground black pepper			
Ground coriander	½ tsp	½ tsp	½ tsp
Single cream	5 oz	5 oz	5 oz
GARNISH			
Garlic bread			

1. Slice the onion, garlic and celery. Add the vegetable oil and place in a glass bowl. Microwave HIGH for 3 minutes.

2. Clean and slice the mushrooms. Add the vegetable stock and seasonings to the onion mixture. Cover with a lid or plate, leaving a gap to allow steam to escape. Microwave HIGH for 10 minutes. Stir once during the cooking process.

3. Remove and process in a food processor for 2 minutes or sieve. Add the cream and the milk and process again.

4. Return the soup to the bowl and microwave MEDIUM for 3 minutes. Serve with garlic bread.

French Onion Soup

Serves 6

INGREDIENTS	Imperial	Metric	American
Butter	*4 oz*	*100 g*	*½ cup*
Onions	*4 large*	*4 large*	*4 large*
Garlic	*4 cloves*	*4 cloves*	*4 cloves*
Brown sugar	*1 tsp*	*1 tsp*	*1 tsp*
Vegetable stock	*1 pt*	*600 ml*	*1 pt*
Sea salt	*1 tsp*	*1 tsp*	*1 tsp*
Freshly ground black pepper			
Nutmeg	*½ tsp*	*½ tsp*	*½ tsp*
GARNISH			
French bread	*6 slices*	*6 slices*	*6 slices*
Cheddar cheese	*4 oz*	*100 g*	*½ cup*

1. Put the butter in a bowl and microwave HIGH for 2 minutes. Add the thinly sliced onions and garlic. Microwave HIGH for 3 minutes. Remove and add the brown sugar. Stir thoroughly and microwave HIGH for a further 3 minutes.

2. Add the vegetable stock and seasonings and microwave HIGH for 10 minutes.

3. In the meantime, grate the cheese and place a little on each slice of bread. Place on a dish and microwave HIGH for 1 minute 30 seconds. Place a cheddar cheese croûton on each bowl of soup and serve piping hot.

Cauliflower and Tomato Soup

Serves 6

INGREDIENTS	Imperial	Metric	American
Butter	2 oz	50 g	1/4 cup
Onions	2 medium	2 medium	2 medium
Garlic	2 cloves	2 cloves	2 cloves
Celery	1 stick	1 stick	1 stick
Cauliflower	1 medium	1 medium	1 medium
Tomatoes	3 medium	3 medium	3 medium
Vegetable stock	1 pt	600 ml	3 cups
Sea salt	1 tsp	1 tsp	1 tsp
Nutmeg	1/2 tsp	1/2 tsp	1/2 tsp
Single cream	2 tbsp	2 tbsp	2 tbsp
Freshly ground black pepper			
GARNISH			
Parmesan Cheese	2 tbsp	2 tbsp	2 tbsp

1. Place the butter in a glass bowl and microwave HIGH for 1 minute. Meanwhile chop the onions, garlic and celery stick. Place in the bowl and microwave HIGH for 3 minutes.

2. Clean and chop the cauliflower and its leaves but removing the core. Skin the tomatoes by placing in a glass bowl, pricking them and covering them with water. Microwave HIGH for 2 minutes. Skin and chop.

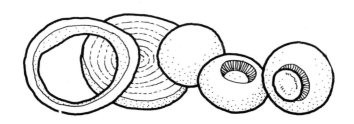

3. Add the chopped cauliflower and tomato to the onion mixture and stir well. Add the vegetable stock and seasonings. Cover with a lid or plate, leaving a gap to allow steam to escape. Microwave HIGH for 5 minutes and stir twice during the cooking process.

4. Remove from the oven, uncover and allow to cool a little. Place in a food processor and process for 2 minutes. Add the cream and process briefly again.

5. Reheat if necessary and microwave MEDIUM for 3 minutes. Serve garnished with Parmesan cheese.

Ginger and Lentil Soup

Serves 6

INGREDIENTS	Imperial	Metric	American
Onions	2 medium	2 medium	2 medium
Garlic	2 cloves	2 cloves	2 cloves
Celery	1 stick	1 stick	1 stick
Root ginger	1/2 in	1.5 cm	1/2 in
Vegetable oil	2 tbsp	2 tbsp	2 tbsp
Red lentils	12 oz	350 g	12 oz
Vegetable stock	1 pt	600 ml	2 1/2 cups
Sea salt			
Freshly ground black pepper			

1. Chop the onions, garlic, celery and root ginger and process in food processor for 1 minute with 1 tbsp of the oil.

2. Place in a glass bowl and add the remaining tablespoon of oil and microwave HIGH for 3 minutes.

3. Thoroughly rinse and pick over the lentils, removing any black seeds or stones which are often there. Add the lentils, vegetable stock and seasoning to the onion mixture and cover with a lid or plate, leaving a gap to allow steam to escape. Microwave HIGH for 12 minutes. Stir twice during the cooking process. Add more liquid if too thick for your taste.

4. A meal in itself served with fresh bread and butter.

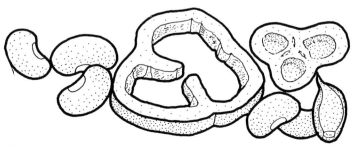

Asparagus Soup

Serves 6

INGREDIENTS	Imperial	Metric	American
Butter	*2 oz*	*50 g*	*¼ cup*
Onion	*1 medium*	*1 medium*	*1 medium*
Garlic	*2 cloves*	*2 cloves*	*2 cloves*
Celery	*1 stick*	*1 stick*	*1 stick*
Fresh asparagus	*½ lb bunch*	*½ lb bunch*	*½ lb bunch*
Vegetable stock	*1 pt*	*600 ml*	*3 cups*
Sea salt	*1 tsp*	*1 tsp*	*1 tsp*
Nutmeg (optional)	*½ tsp*	*½ tsp*	*½ tsp*
Single cream	*2 tbsp*	*2 tbsp*	*2 tbsp*
Freshly ground black pepper			

GARNISH
Freshly chopped parsley

1. Place the butter in a glass bowl and microwave HIGH for 1 minute. Chop the onion, garlic and the celery stick and add to the butter. Stir together. Microwave HIGH for 3 minutes.

2. Scrape the asparagus and remove the tough end of each stick. Chop into 2 cm/1 in long pieces. Add to the other vegetables with the vegetable stock and seasonings. Cover with a lid or plate, leaving a gap to allow steam to escape. Microwave HIGH for 15 minutes stirring twice during the cooking process.

3. Remove from the oven and allow to cool slightly. Place in a food processor and process for 2 minutes until very smooth. Add the cream and the pepper and process again briefly.

4. Reheat if necessary. Microwave MEDIUM for 3 minutes. Serve garnished with freshly chopped parsley.

Spicy Pumpkin Soup

Serves 8

INGREDIENTS	Imperial	Metric	American
Vegetable oil	2 tbsp	2 tbsp	2 tbsp
Onions	2 medium	2 medium	2 medium
Garlic	3 cloves	3 cloves	3 cloves
Celery	1 stick	1 stick	1 stick
Hot green chilli	1 small	1 small	1 small
Cardamon seeds	6	6	6
Cumin seeds	1 tsp	1 tsp	1 tsp
Fresh pumpkin	1/4 medium	1/4 medium	1/4 medium
Tomatoes	3 medium	3 medium	3 medium
Tomato purée	2 tbsp	2 tbsp	2 tbsp
Vegetable stock	1 pt	600 ml	3 cups
Sea salt	1 tsp	1 tsp	1 tsp
Chinese 5 spice	1/2 tsp	1/2 tsp	1/2 tsp
Paprika	1/2 tsp	1/2 tsp	1/2 tsp
Tabasco sauce	4 drops	4 drops	4 drops
Freshly ground black pepper			

GARNISH
Freshly chopped
coriander/parsley

1. Place the vegetable oil in a glass bowl and add the chopped onions, garlic and celery. Add the chopped chilli with the seeds removed and add the cardamon and cumin seeds. Microwave HIGH for 3 minutes.

2. Peel, deseed and chop the pumpkin into small cubes. (Unsweetened tinned pumpkin can be used instead of fresh.) Prick the tomatoes and place in a bowl of water. Microwave HIGH for 2 minutes. Cool and remove the skins from the tomatoes. Chop and add with the pumpkin to the onion mixture. Add the tomato purée, vegetable stock and

seasonings. Cover with a lid or plate, leaving a gap to allow steam to escape. Microwave HIGH for 15 minutes stirring twice during cooking.

3. Cook slightly then beat with a whisk or briefly process in a food processor. Serve garnished with fresh coriander or parsley.

Watercress Soup

Serves 6

INGREDIENTS	Imperial	Metric	American
Onion	1 medium	1 medium	1 medium
Garlic	2 cloves	2 cloves	2 cloves
Celery	1 stick	1 stick	1 stick
Potato	1 large	1 large	1 large
Vegetable oil	2 tbsp	2 tbsp	2 tbsp
Watercress	2 bunches	2 bunches	2 bunches
Vegetable stock	1 pt	600 ml	1 pt
Sea salt	1 tsp	1 tsp	1 tsp
Nutmeg	$\frac{1}{2}$ tsp	$\frac{1}{2}$ tsp	$\frac{1}{2}$ tsp
Single cream	2 tbsp	2 tbsp	2 tbsp
Freshly ground black pepper			

GARNISH
Watercress

1. Slice the onion, garlic and celery and place in a glass bowl. Peel and cube the potato and add to the vegetables. Sprinkle over the vegetable oil and microwave HIGH for 3 minutes.

2. Clean and chop the watercress removing the larger stalks. Reserve some of the smaller leaves for the garnish. Add with the vegetable stock and seasonings to the bowl. Cover with a lid or plate, leaving a gap to allow steam to escape. Microwave HIGH for 10 minutes. Stir once during cooking.

3. Remove from the oven and allow to rest. Add the cream and freshly ground pepper. Process in a food processor for 2 minutes or sieve.

4. Place in the glass bowl again and cover as before. Microwave MEDIUM for 3 minutes. Garnish with watercress. Can be served cold.

Slimming Vegetable Soup

Serves 8

INGREDIENTS	Imperial	Metric	American
Onion	1 medium	1 medium	1 medium
Garlic	2 cloves	2 cloves	2 cloves
Carrots	2 medium	2 medium	2 medium
Courgettes	2 medium	2 medium	2 medium
Red pepper	1 medium	1 medium	1 medium
Brussel sprouts	3 small	3 small	3 small
Mushrooms	4 medium	4 medium	4 medium
Vegetable stock	1 pt	600 ml	2½ cups
Sea salt	1 tsp	1 tsp	1 tsp
Freshly ground black pepper			
Mixed spice	½ tsp	½ tsp	½ tsp
Cheddar cheese, grated	4 oz	100 g	½ cup

1. Chop and slice the vegetables very finely, preferably cutting the carrots and the courgettes on the diagonal. Place all the ingredients except the cheese in a glass bowl.

2. Place in the microwave and microwave HIGH for 5 minutes. Remove and stir. Replace and microwave HIGH for 5 minutes, each time covering with a lid or plate, leaving a gap to allow steam to escape. The vegetables should be quite crunchy.

3. Sprinkle with grated Cheddar cheese to serve.

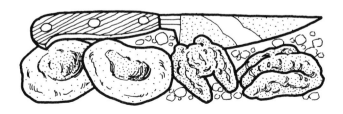

29

2 STARTERS

Stuffed Tomatoes

Serves 4

INGREDIENTS	Imperial	Metric	American
Beef tomatoes	4 large	4 large	4 large
Onion	1 medium	1 medium	1 medium
Garlic	2 cloves	2 cloves	2 cloves
Vegetable oil	2 tsp	2 tsp	2 tsp
Cooked rice	4 tbsp	4 tbsp	4 tbsp
Sea salt	1 tsp	1 tsp	1 tsp
Nutmeg	1/2 tsp	1/2 tsp	1/2 tsp
Vegetable stock	2 tbsp	2 tbsp	2 tbsp
GARNISH			
Roasted sesame seeds	4 tsp	4 tsp	4 tsp
Watercress			

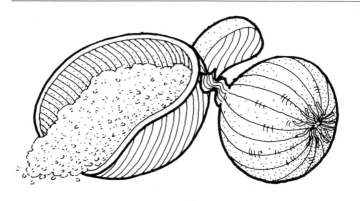

1. Cut the tops off the tomatoes and carefully remove the seeds and the fibres. Place the tomatoes on a glass dish suitable for microwave.

2. Chop the onion and garlic quite finely and mix with the tomatoes. Place in a glass bowl and add the vegetable oil. Microwave HIGH uncovered for 3 minutes. Remove and cool slightly. Add the cooked rice (preferably brown), salt and nutmeg and mix together.

3. Stuff the tomatoes with the mixture replacing the tops. Microwave MEDIUM for 6 minutes. Remove and garnish with roasted sesame seeds and watercress.

Stuffed Red Peppers

Serves 4

INGREDIENTS	Imperial	Metric	American
Red peppers	4 medium	4 medium	4 medium
Onion	1 medium	1 medium	1 medium
Garlic	2 cloves	2 cloves	2 cloves
Mushrooms	8 medium	8 medium	8 medium
Vegetable oil	2 tbsp	2 tbsp	2 tbsp
Cooked rice	4 tbsp	4 tbsp	4 tbsp
Sunflower seeds	2 tbsp	2 tbsp	2 tbsp
Sea salt	1 tsp	1 tsp	1 tsp
Freshly ground black pepper			
Ground cumin	½ tsp	½ tsp	½ tsp
Vegetable stock	4 tbsp	4 tbsp	4 tbspA5.5

1. Halve the peppers. Wash and remove seeds and internal fibres. Place back together in a glass dish suitable for microwave. Put to one side.

2. Slice the onions, garlic and mushrooms quite finely. Sprinkle with oil and put in a glass bowl and cover with a lid or plate, leaving a gap to allow steam to escape. Microwave HIGH for 3 minutes.

3. Remove from the oven and add the cooked rice (preferably brown rice), sunflower seeds and seasonings. Stuff the peppers with this mixture. Carefully put the two halves together.

4. Sprinkle the vegetable stock over the peppers and microwave HIGH for 10 minutes.

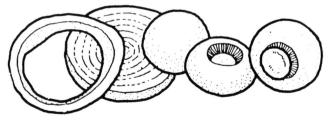

Tofu with Bean Sprouts

Serves 4

INGREDIENTS	Imperial	Metric	American
Tofu	*4 oz*	*100 g*	*4 oz*
Bean sprouts	*2 oz*	*50 g*	*2 oz*
Red pepper	*1 medium*	*1 medium*	*1 medium*
Onion	*1 medium*	*1 medium*	*1 medium*
Garlic	*2 cloves*	*2 cloves*	*2 cloves*
Vegetable oil	*2 tsp*	*2 tsp*	*2 tsp*
Sea salt	*1 tsp*	*1 tsp*	*1 tsp*

GARNISH
Parsley, chopped
Freshly ground
* black pepper*

1. Chop the tofu into 1 cm/½ in pieces and place in a glass bowl suitable for microwave.

2. Thoroughly clean the bean sprouts and place in the glass bowl. Chop the red pepper, onion and garlic quite finely. Place in a glass bowl and sprinkle with the oil. Microwave HIGH for 3 minutes.

3. Add the onion mixture to the bean sprouts and combine well together. Sprinkle with salt. Microwave HIGH for 10 minutes. Pile on individual plates and garnish with chopped parsley and ground pepper. Serve with fresh brown bread and butter.

Aubergine Parmesan

Serves 6

INGREDIENTS	Imperial	Metric	American
Aubergine	1 medium	1 medium	1 medium
Shallot	1	1	1
Garlic	2 cloves	2 cloves	2 cloves
Lemon juice	1 tbsp	1 tbsp	1 tbsp
Greek yoghurt	2 tbsp	2 tbsp	2 tbsp
Sea salt	1 tsp	1 tsp	1 tsp
Freshly ground black pepper			
Vegetable oil	2 tbsp	2 tbsp	2 tbsp
French bread	6 slices	6 slices	6 slices
Parmesan cheese	4 oz	100 g	½ cup

GARNISH
Fresh watercress

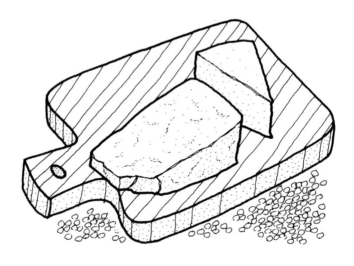

1. Brush the aubergine with oil, prick with a fork and place on a plate. Microwave HIGH for 10 minutes. Cool slightly. Scoop out flesh and place in a food processor with the chopped shallot and garlic. Process for 1 minute. Add the lemon juice, yoghurt and seasoning and process again for 1 minute. If you do not have a food processor, blend all the ingredients together with a wooden spoon.

2. Put the oil on a plate and dip the bread into it covering both sides. Pile the aubergine mixture on to the bread and sprinkle with Parmesan cheese. Microwave HIGH for 1 minute and 30 seconds. Serve immediately. Garnish with fresh watercress.

Mushroom Kebab

Serves 4

INGREDIENTS	Imperial	Metric	American
Field mushrooms	½ lb	225 g	8 oz
Onion	1 large	1 large	1 large
Red pepper	1 large	1 large	1 large
Vegetable oil	1 tbsp	1 tbsp	1 tbsp
Sea salt	1 tsp	1 tsp	1 tsp
Lemon juice	½ lemon	½ lemon	½ lemon

GARNISH
Chopped parsley

1. Select mushrooms of a similar size, preferably about
3 cm/1 ½ in in diameter. Wipe clean with a damp cloth. Do
not immerse in water. Cut the onion in half and then in
quarters, making quite large pieces. Cut the red pepper into
similar pieces. Place the mushrooms, onion and red pepper
alternately on wooden kebab sticks (essential for microwave
ovens). Pack closely together and place on a round dish
suitable for microwave. Sprinkle with the vegetable oil, salt and
lemon juice.

2. Cook HI-SPEED at 250°C for 12 minutes turning twice
during cooking, basting each time with the juices. Or microwave
HIGH for 4 minutes. Garnish.

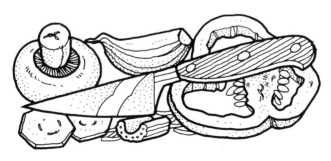

Ratatouille

Serves 6

INGREDIENTS	Imperial	Metric	American
Olive oil	2 tbsp	2 tbsp	2 tbsp
Onions, sliced	2 medium	2 medium	2 medium
Garlic, chopped	2 cloves	2 cloves	2 cloves
Aubergines	2 medium	2 medium	2 medium
Green pepper	1	1	1
Red pepper	1	1	1
Chilli (optional)	1	1	1
Courgettes	3	3	3
Can of tomatoes	1½ lb	750 g	1½ lb
Paprika	1 tsp	1 tsp	1 tsp
Basil	1 tsp	1 tsp	1 tsp
Fresh chives	1 tbsp	1 tbsp	1 tbsp
Tomato purée	1 tbsp	1 tbsp	1 tbsp
Brown sugar	1 tsp	1 tsp	1 tsp
Sea salt	1 tsp	1 tsp	1 tsp
Freshly ground black pepper			

1. Heat the oil in a frying pan and gently fry the onions and the garlic until just translucent. Slice the aubergine and lay out on a tray. Sprinkle with salt and allow to sweat for 15 minutes. Turn over and repeat on the other side. Scrape the salt off and chop. Add to the onions. Chop the peppers, chilli and courgettes and add to the frying pan.

2. In a casserole suitable for the microwave, combine the remaining ingredients, chopping the tinned tomatoes into small pieces. Add the vegetables from the frying pan and stir well. Cover the casserole and microwave **HIGH** for 5 minutes. Stir. Microwave **MEDIUM** for 10 minutes.

Spinach Florentine

Serves 6

INGREDIENTS	Imperial	Metric	American
Spinach	8 oz	200 g	3 cups
Butter	1 oz	25 g	1 oz
Plain flour	1 oz	25 g	1 oz
Milk	1/2 pt	275 ml	1 1/2 cups
Mature Cheddar cheese	2 oz	50 g	1 cup
Eggs	4 medium	4 medium	4 medium
Sea salt	1/2 tsp	1/2 tsp	1/2 tsp
Freshly ground nutmeg			
Freshly ground black pepper			
GARNISH			
Parmesan cheese	2 tbsp	2 tbsp	2 tbsp

1. Thoroughly clean the spinach and remove the stems. Place in a glass bowl. Cover with a lid or plate, leaving a gap to allow steam to escape. Microwave HIGH for 8 minutes. Cook and uncover. Squeeze out excess water and place in a greased flan dish.

2. Make the cheese sauce by placing the butter in a pint glass measuring jug. Microwave HIGH for 1 minute. Remove from the oven and throughly mix in the flour. Add the milk and mix again. Microwave HIGH for 3 minutes stirring twice during cooking. Add the cheese and microwave for a further minute. Stir thoroughly.

3. Break the eggs on to the spinach and season with salt, pepper and nutmeg to taste. Pour over the cheese sauce and cook HI-SPEED at 250°C for 6 minutes or until the eggs are the desired consistency. Or microwave HIGH for 2 minutes, then grill to brown, if liked.

4. Garnish with a sprinkle of Parmesan cheese.

Note: Alternatively, individual ramekins can be made.

Leeks à la Grecque

Serves 6

INGREDIENTS	Imperial	Metric	American
Leeks	*6 medium*	*6 medium*	*6 medium*
Vegetable oil	*1 tbsp*	*1 tbsp*	*1 tbsp*
Onion	*1 medium*	*1 medium*	*1 medium*
Garlic	*2 cloves*	*2 cloves*	*2 cloves*
Mushrooms	*4 oz*	*100 g*	*1 cup*
Tin of tomatoes	*14oz*	*400 gr*	*14 oz*
Tomato purée	*2 tbsp*	*2 tbsp*	*2 tbsp*
Mustard	*1 tsp*	*1 tsp*	*1 tsp*
Sea salt			
Freshly ground black pepper			

1. Slice the leeks in two lengthwise and clean thoroughly discarding the outside leaves. Place in a glass bowl. Sprinkle with water and microwave HIGH for 8 minutes. Cool.

2. Place the oil in a glass bowl and add the chopped onion, garlic and sliced mushrooms. Microwave HIGH for 3 minutes.

3. Process the tinned tomatoes in a food processor for 2 minutes with the tomato puree and the seasonings.

4. Add to the onion mixture and stir thoroughly. Cover with a lid or plate, leaving a gap to allow steam to escape. Microwave HIGH for 8 minutes. Cool.

5. Serve the cold leeks with the cold sauce and hot French bread.

Mushrooms in Cream and Brandy

Serves 6

INGREDIENTS	Imperial	Metric	American
Field mushrooms	*12*	*12*	*12*
Butter	*1 oz*	*25 g*	*1 oz*
Onion	*1 medium*	*1 medium*	*1 medium*
Double cream	*5 fl oz*	*150 ml*	*5 fl oz*
Brandy	*2 tbsp*	*2 tbsp*	*2 tbsp*

GARNISH
Freshly chopped parsley

1. Place the washed mushrooms top side down on a plate. Sprinkle with water and microwave HIGH for 8 minutes.

2. Melt the butter in the microwave on HIGH for 1 minute. Add the finely chopped onion and microwave HIGH for 3 minutes.

3. Add the double cream and the brandy by pouring over the cooked mushrooms. Sprinkle with freshly chopped parsley.

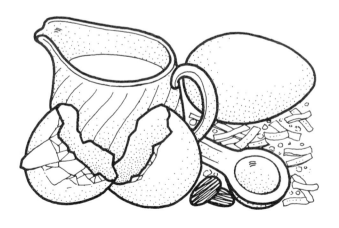

Nut Balls and Tomato Sauce

Serves 6

INGREDIENTS	Imperial	Metric	American
Mixed nuts	4 oz	100 g	1 cup
Brown bread	4 oz	100 g	1 cup
Onions	2 medium	2 medium	2 medium
Garlic	2 cloves	2 cloves	2 cloves
Vegetable oil	1 tbsp	1 tbsp	1 tbsp
Marmite	1 tsp	1 tsp	1 tsp
Water	4 tbsp	4 tbsp	4 tbsp
Sea salt	2 tsp	2 tsp	2 tsp
Roasted sesame seeds	2 oz	50 g	1/4 cup
SAUCE			
Butter or			
margarine	1 oz	25 g	1 oz
Onions	2 medium	2 medium	2 medium
Garlic	2 cloves	2 cloves	2 cloves
Tin of tomatoes	14 oz	400 g	14 oz
Tomato purée	2 tbsp	2 tbsp	2 tbsp
Sea salt	1 tsp	1 tsp	1 tsp
Basil	1 tsp	1 tsp	1 tsp

1. Grind the mixed nuts in a coffee grinder in small quantities with the bread and place to one side. Chop by hand if larger pieces of nuts are preferred.

2. Chop the onions and the garlic quite finely and place in a glass bowl. Sprinkle with the vegetable oil. Place in the oven and microwave HIGH for 3 minutes.

3. Combine the onion mixture with the nuts. Make a vegetable stock by adding 4 tbsp of water to the marmite. Stir thoroughly and add to the mixture. The mixture should not be too wet.

4. Take a good teaspoonful of the mixture and make into a ball in the palm of the hand. Roll in the sesame seeds and place in

a plate suitable for microwave and the oven. Cook **HI-SPEED** for 10 minutes at 250°C. Or microwave **HIGH** for 3½ minutes.

5. To make the sauce melt the butter in a glass bowl in the microwave on **HIGH** for 1 minute. Add the finely chopped onion and garlic and microwave **HIGH** for 3 minutes. Place the tinned tomatoes, tomato purée, salt and basil in a food processor and process for 2 minutes.

6. Combine with the onion mixture in the glass bowl. Cover with a lid or plate, leaving a gap to allow steam to escape.

7. While the nut balls are cooling a little, microwave the sauce on **HIGH** for 5 minutes and pour over the nut balls.

8. Serve with fresh wholemeal bread.

Corn on the Cob and Garlic Butter

Serves 6

INGREDIENTS	Imperial	Metric	American
Fresh corn cobs	6	6	6
Butter	*4 oz*	*100 g*	*4 oz*
Garlic	*2 cloves*	*2 cloves*	*2 cloves*
Sea salt			
Freshly ground black pepper			
GARNISH			
French bread			

1. Wash the freshly picked corn and leave the husks on them. Place the corn on a large plate and microwave HIGH for 8 minutes, cooking three at a time.

2. Place the butter in a large measuring jug and crush the garlic cloves into the butter. Season with salt and pepper. Microwave HIGH for 2 minutes.

3. Remove the husks and serve with a small bowl of the garlic butter with hot French bread.

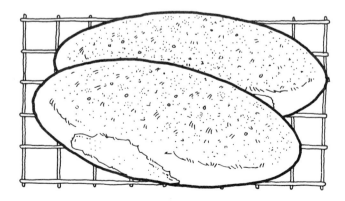

Mixed Vegetable Kebab

Serves 4

INGREDIENTS	Imperial	Metric	American
Red pepper	1 large	1 large	1 large
Courgettes	2 medium	2 medium	2 medium
Parsnip	1 medium	1 medium	1 medium
Mushrooms	8	8	8
Onion	1 medium	1 medium	1 medium
Carrots	2 medium	2 medium	2 medium
Potato	1 medium	1 medium	1 medium
Vegetable stock	4 tbsp	4 tbsp	4 tbsp
Cheddar cheese	4 oz	100 g	4 oz
Sea salt			
Freshly ground black pepper			
GARNISH			
Brown rice	4 oz	100 g	4 oz

Note: It is important to use wooden kebab sticks for this recipe as metal ones will make the microwave flash.
1. Wash and prepare the vegetables. Cut into suitable pieces to place on the kebab sticks. The courgettes and carrots should be cut diagonally. The mushrooms should remain whole. Place alternately on sticks and pack tightly. Lay the kebabs on a circular dish and sprinkle with vegetable stock.

2. Cook HI-SPEED 250°C for 12 minutes turning twice during cooking. Or microwave HIGH for 4 minutes. Remove and sprinkle with Cheddar cheese. Cook HI-SPEED for a further 5 minutes. Or microwave HIGH for 2 minutes, then grill to brown, if liked. Serve on a bed of brown rice.

Leek and Walnut Pancake

Serves 6

INGREDIENTS	Imperial	Metric	American
PANCAKE BATTER			
Plain flour	*4 oz*	*100 g*	*1 cup*
Sea salt	*1 tsp*	*1 tsp*	*1 tsp*
Milk	*8 fl oz*	*250 ml*	*1 cup*
Egg	*1 medium*	*1 medium*	*1 medium*
Egg yolk	*1*	*1*	*1*
Vegetable oil for frying	*1 tsp*	*1 tsp*	*1 tsp*
FILLING			
Vegetable oil	*1 tsp*	*1 tsp*	*1 tsp*
Leeks	*2 medium*	*2 medium*	*2 medium*
Soured cream	*5 fl oz*	*150 ml*	*5 fl oz*
Walnuts	*4 oz*	*100 g*	*1 cup*
Cornflour	*1 oz*	*25 g*	*1 oz*
Milk	*2 tbsp*	*2 tbsp*	*2 tbsp*
Sea salt			
Freshly ground black pepper			
GARNISH			
Parmesan cheese	*2 oz*	*50 g*	*2 oz*

1. Sift the flour and salt into a bowl. Add the milk, egg, egg yolk and oil and whisk until smooth. Leave to stand for 1 hour.

2. Lightly oil a 15 cm/6 in pancake frying pan and heat. Pour in a little batter, swirl round and cook for 2 minutes then turn and cook the other side for about 30 seconds. Continue to make 11 more pancakes, pile on top of each other and put to one side.

3. Place the vegetable oil in the glass bowl and add the thoroughly cleaned and chopped leeks. Microwave HIGH for 3 minutes. Remove and cool a little.

4. Add the soured cream and chopped walnuts. Mix the cornflour with the milk and add with the seasonings to the mixture. Microwave HIGH for 3 minutes, stirring twice during cooking.

5. Stuff the pancakes with 2 tablespoons each of the leek and walnut mixture. Place on a large plate and microwave HIGH for 3 minutes.

6. Serve garnished with Parmesan cheese.

Note: Pancakes are more successful made in the conventional way on the hob. They freeze very well or can be bought ready-made. It is well worth making a batch for freezing as they are excellent reheated in the microwave.

Spinach, Parsnip and Carrot Terrine

Serves 6

INGREDIENTS	Imperial	Metric	American
Spinach	1 lb	500 g	1 lb
Eggs	2 medium	2 medium	2 medium
Single cream	2 tbsp	2 tbsp	2 tbsp
Nutmeg	1/2 tsp	1/2 tsp	1/2 tsp
Sea salt			
Freshly ground black pepper			
Parsnip	8 oz	250 g	8 oz
Eggs	2 medium	2 medium	2 medium
Single cream	2 tbsp	2 tbsp	2 tbsp
Carrot	8 oz	250 g	8 oz
Eggs	2 medium	2 medium	2 medium
Single cream	2 tbsp	2 tbsp	2 tbsp
GARNISH			
Watercress			

1. Prepare each vegetable separately. Clean the spinach, remove the stems and place in a bowl without water. Microwave HIGH for 8 minutes. Cool. Process the spinach in a food processor with the eggs, cream, nutmeg and seasonings for 2 minutes. Pour into the bottom of a greased casserole.

2. Peel and slice the parsnips. Place in a bowl and add 2 tablespoons of water and microwave for 10 minutes. Cool. Place the drained parsnips in the food processor with the eggs, cream and seasonings. Spoon gently on top of the spinach making a parsnip layer.

3. Peel and slice the carrots. Add 2 tablespoons of water and microwave HIGH for 10 minutes. Drain and cool. Place in a food processor with the eggs, cream and seasonings. Process for 2 minutes. Spoon gently on to the parsnip layer.

4. Place in the microwave on MEDIUM for 10 minutes. Allow to stand for 2 minutes. If brave, turn out. Garnish with fresh watercress.

Stuffed Vine Leaves

Serves 4

INGREDIENTS	Imperial	Metric	American
Boiling water			
Vine leaves	*12*	*12*	*12*
Vegetable oil	*1 tbsp*	*1 tbsp*	*1 tbsp*
Onion	*1 medium*	*1 medium*	*1 medium*
Garlic	*2 cloves*	*2 cloves*	*2 cloves*
Celery	*1 stick*	*1 stick*	*1 stick*
Raisins	*2 oz*	*50 g*	*2 oz*
Cashew nuts	*2 oz*	*50 g*	*2 oz*
Cooked rice	*2 oz*	*50 g*	*2 oz*
Vegetable stock	*4 tbsp*	*4 tbsp*	*4 tbsp*
GARNISH			
Watercress			

---

1. If vacuum packed vine leaves are used, separate 12 good large ones and place in a bowl of boiling water. Microwave HIGH for 5 minutes. Drain.

2. Place the vegetable oil in a glass bowl and add the chopped onion, garlic and celery. Microwave HIGH for 3 minutes. Add the raisins, chopped cashews, rice and vegetable stock and mix together.

3. Stuff each vine leaf with a good teaspoonful of the mixture and place on a plate. Microwave HIGH for 5 minutes.

4. Serve garnished with watercress.

3 MAIN COURSES

Parsnip and Cheese Soufflé

Serves 6

INGREDIENTS	Imperial	Metric	American
Parsnips	3 medium	3 medium	3 medium
Onion	1 medium	1 medium	1 medium
Garlic	2 cloves	2 cloves	2 cloves
Vegetable stock	4 tbsp	4 tbsp	4 tbsp
Butter	2 oz	50 g	1/2 cup
Flour	2 oz	50 g	1/2 cup
Milk	1/2 pt	300 ml	1 1/2 cups
Cheddar Cheese	4 oz	100 g	1 cup
Cream	2 tbsp	2 tbsp	2 tbsp
Sea salt	1/2 tsp	1/2 tsp	1/2 tsp
Nutmeg	1/2 tsp	1/2 tsp	1/2 tsp
Freshly ground black pepper			
Eggs, separated	4	4	4

1. Slice the parsnips, onions and garlic quite thinly and place in a bowl with 4 tbsp of vegetable stock. Microwave HIGH for 10 minutes. Remove. Place in a food processor or liquidiser and process for 2 minutes. Cool.

2. Place the butter in a glass bowl and microwave HIGH for 1 minute. Stir in the flour and add the milk. Whisk to thoroughly incorporate the flour and microwave HIGH for 3 minutes stirring regularly. Combine with parsnip mixture and add the grated Cheddar cheese, cream, seasonings and egg yolks. Whisk the egg whites until they form stiff peaks. Fold into parsnip mixture and place gently in a large soufflé dish which has been well greased.

3. Cook on HI-SPEED, 250°C for 12 minutes. Or microwave LOW for 10 minutes, then sprinkle with extra grated nutmeg. This soufflé can be prepared an hour ahead of time and cooked just prior to serving.

4. Serve with a watercress salad.

Vegetarian Hot Pot

Serves 8 (4)

INGREDIENTS		Imperial	Metric	American
Onions	1	2 medium	2 medium	2 medium
Garlic	1	2 cloves	2 cloves	2 cloves
Carrots	1	2 medium	2 medium	2 medium
Vegetable oil	1	2 tbsp	2 tbsp	2 tbsp
Cardamon seeds ?	3 . 6	6	6	
Parsnip 1	small 1 medium	1 medium	1 medium	
Potato	medium 1 large	1 large	1 large	
Turnips	1	2 small	2 small	2 small
Courgettes	1	2 medium	2 medium	2 medium
Red pepper	1	1 large	1 large	1 large
Hot pepper ?		1 small	1 small	1 small
Curry powder	½ 1 tsp	1 tsp	1 tsp	
Sea salt		1 tsp	1 tsp	1 tsp
Freshly ground black pepper				
Vegetable stock	½ 1 pt	575 ml	2½ cups	
Cornflour	½ 1 tbsp	1 tbsp	1 tbsp	
GARNISH				
Sunflower seeds	? 2 .4 tbsp	4 tbsp	4 tbsp	

1. Chop and slice the onions, garlic and carrots and place in a glass bowl with the vegetable oil and cardamon seeds. Microwave HIGH for 3 minutes.

2. Prepare the remaining ingredients by chopping them and dicing the parsnip, potato and turnips. Add with the seasonings to the onion mixture and place in casserole. Mix the cornflour with a little of the vegetable stock then add to the bowl. Microwave HIGH for 15 minutes, stirring every 5 minutes.

3. Remove and sprinkle with sunflower seeds and microwave HIGH for 1 minute.

Chinese Vegetable Stir-fry

Serves 6

INGREDIENTS	Imperial	Metric	American
Onion	1 medium	1 medium	1 medium
Garlic	2 cloves	2 cloves	2 cloves
Parsnip	1 medium	1 medium	1 medium
Carrots	2 medium	2 medium	2 medium
Vegetable oil	2 tbsp	2 tbsp	2 tbsp
Cardamon seeds	6	6	6
Chinese cabbage	1/2	1/2	1/2
Bean sprouts	2 oz	50 g	2 oz
Mange tout	12	12	12
Vegetable stock	4 tbsp	4 tbsp	4 tbsp
Sesame oil	1 tsp	1 tsp	1 tsp
Soya sauce	1 tsp	1 tsp	1 tsp
Chinese 5 spice	1 tsp	1 tsp	1 tsp
Sea salt			
Freshly ground black pepper			
GARNISH			
Grûyére cheese	4 oz	100 g	4 oz

1. Chop and slice the onion and garlic quite finely. Slice the carrot and the parsnip on the diagonal and place in a glass bowl with the vegetable oil and cardamon seeds. Microwave HIGH for 3 minutes.

2. Chop the Chinese cabbage. Clean the bean sprouts. Top and tail the mange tout and add to the glass bowl with the remaining ingredients and seasonings. Cover with a lid or plate, leaving a gap to allow steam to escape. Microwave HIGH for 10 minutes stirring once during the cooking process.

3. Serve garnished with grated Grûyére cheese for a healthy wholesome meal.

Spinach Ricotta Layer

Serves 6

INGREDIENTS	Imperial	Metric	American
Spinach	12 oz	350 g	12 oz
Sea salt	1 tsp	1 tsp	1 tsp
Eggs	3 medium	3 medium	3 medium
Cream	2 tbsp	2 tbsp	2 tbsp
Mushrooms	4 oz	100 g	4 oz
Butter	2 oz	50 g	2 oz
Ricotta cheese	4 oz	100 g	4 oz
Sea salt	1 tsp	1 tsp	1 tsp
Freshly ground black pepper			
GARNISH			
Roasted split almonds	2 oz	50 g	2 oz

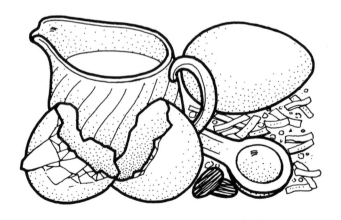

1. Clean the spinach and remove the stems. Place in a glass bowl. Sprinkle with salt. Microwave HIGH for 8 minutes. Rest for 2 minutes. Combine the eggs and the cream and mix with the spinach. Divide the mixture into two.

2. Melt the butter in the microwave on HIGH for 1 minute. Add the cleaned, sliced mushrooms and microwave HIGH for 4 minutes. Rest for 2 minutes then combine the ricotta cheese with the mushrooms seasoning to taste.

3. In a loaf dish, place half the spinach mixture then add the ricotta and mushroom layer. Finally add the last spinach layer.

4. Bake at HI-SPEED for 10 minutes at 250°C. Or microwave MEDIUM for 6 minutes. Rest, turn out and garnish with roasted almonds.

Spanish Omelette

Serves 6

INGREDIENTS	Imperial	Metric	American
Butter or margarine	*2 oz*	*50 g*	*2 oz*
Onions	*2 medium*	*2 medium*	*2 medium*
Garlic	*2 cloves*	*2 cloves*	*2 cloves*
Red pepper	*1 large*	*1 large*	*1 large*
Potatoes	*2 large*	*2 large*	*2 large*
Eggs	*4 large*	*4 large*	*4 large*
Milk	*4 tbsp*	*4 tbsp*	*4 tbsp*
Sea salt	*1 tsp*	*1 tsp*	*1 tsp*
Cheddar cheese	*2 oz*	*50 g*	*2 oz*
Paprika	*1 tsp*	*1 tsp*	*1 tsp*
Freshly ground black pepper			

GARNISH
Freshly chopped parsley

1. Place the butter in a glass bowl and microwave HIGH for 1 minute. Chop the onion, garlic and red pepper. Peel and slice the potatoes quite thinly. Place in the bowl, turn over the ingredients so they all have a little butter on them. Cover with a lid or plate, leaving a gap to allow steam to escape. Microwave HIGH for 5 minutes.

2. Remove from the oven and place in a flan dish being sure that the potato is evenly distributed.

3. Combine the eggs and milk then add the salt and cheese. Pour over the vegetables and sprinkle with paprika and freshly ground black pepper.

4. Cook HI-SPEED for 8 minutes or until the omelette is set. Or microwave MEDIUM for 6 minutes. Garnish with freshly chopped parsley.

Cauliflower and Celery Cheese

Serves 6

INGREDIENTS	Imperial	Metric	American
Cauliflower	1 lb	450 g	1 lb
Celery	1 lb	450 g	1 lb
Water	4 tbsp	4 tbsp	4 tbsp
Butter	2 oz	50 g	1/4 cup
Plain flour	2 oz	50 g	1/4 cup
Milk	1 pt	600 ml	2 1/2 cups
Cheddar cheese, grated	4 oz	100 g	1/2 cup
Sunflower seeds	2 oz	50 g	1/4 cup
Sea salt	1 tsp	1 tsp	1 tsp
Freshly ground black pepper			

1. Wash and clean the cauliflower and celery and cut into florets and 4 cm/2 in pieces. Place in a casserole with the water. Put the lid on the casserole and microwave HIGH for 10 minutes. Drain.

2. Place the butter in a glass bowl and microwave HIGH for 1 minute. Blend in the flour and add the milk, salt and pepper. Whisk. Microwave HIGH for 3 minutes whisking every minute. Add the Cheddar cheese and microwave HIGH for another minute.

3. Pour the cheese sauce over the cauliflower and celery. Sprinkle the sunflower seeds on the top and cook on HI-SPEED uncovered for 8 minutes. Or microwave HIGH for 3 minutes.

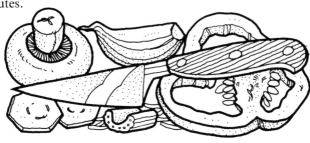

Leek and Potato Pie

Serves 8

INGREDIENTS	Imperial	Metric	American
PASTRY			
Wholemeal flour	*8 oz*	*225 g*	*2 cups*
Sea salt	*1 tsp*	*1 tsp*	*1 tsp*
Butter or margarine	*2 oz*	*50 g*	*¼ cup*
Vegetable lard	*2 oz*	*50 g*	*¼ cup*
Iced water	*4 fl oz*	*120 ml*	*½ cup*
FILLING			
Onions	*2 medium*	*2 medium*	*2 medium*
Garlic	*2 cloves*	*2 cloves*	*2 cloves*
Leeks	*2 medium*	*2 medium*	*2 medium*
Potatoes	*2 medium*	*2 medium*	*2 medium*
Eggs	*3 medium*	*3 medium*	*3 medium*
Cream	*3 tbsp*	*3 tbsp*	*3 tbsp*
Sea salt	*1 tsp*	*1 tsp*	*1 tsp*
Paprika	*½ tsp*	*½ tsp*	*½ tsp*
Cumin seeds	*1 tsp*	*1 tsp*	*1 tsp*
Freshly ground black pepper			
GARNISH			
Mixed green salad			

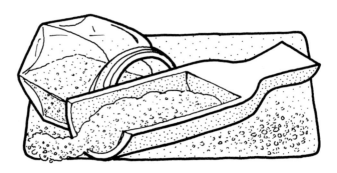

1. Make the pastry by sifting the flour and salt into a bowl. Cut in the butter or margarine and lard. Add sufficient water to make a soft dough. Form into a ball and leave to rest in the fridge for 30 minutes.

2. Slice the onions, garlic, leeks and potatoes. Place in a glass bowl and sprinkle with water. Microwave HIGH for 7 minutes.

3. Roll out the pastry and line a flan dish. Arrange the vegetables in the dish with a top layer of potatoes.

4. Combine the eggs, cream and salt and pour over the vegetables. Sprinkle with cumin seeds, paprika, and freshly ground black pepper. Make a lattice pattern on the top with remaining pastry. Bake on HI-SPEED for 20 minutes at 250°C. Or microwave HIGH for 7 minutes, then sprinkle with extra paprika.

Cabbage and Apple Casserole

Serves 8

INGREDIENTS	Imperial	Metric	American
Onion, sliced	2 medium	2 medium	2 medium
Red cabbage, chopped	8 oz	225 g	2 cups
White cabbage, chopped	8 oz	225 g	2 cups
Red Delicious apples, sliced	2 medium	2 medium	2 medium
Red wine	4 tbsp	4 tbsp	4 tbsp
Red wine sugar	4 tbsp	4 tbsp	4 tbsp
Soft brown sugar	2 tbsp	2 tbsp	2 tbsp
Pine nuts or walnuts	2 tbsp	2 tbsp	2 tbsp
Raisins or sultanas	2 tbsp	2 tbsp	2 tbsp
Nutmeg	1/2 tsp	1/2 tsp	1/2 tsp
Ground cumin	1/2 tsp	1/2 tsp	1/2 tsp
Mixed spice	1/2 tsp	1/2 tsp	1/2 tsp
Salt			
Pepper			

1. Place the sliced onion in a large casserole and microwave HIGH for 3 minutes. Remove and add all the remaining ingredients.

2. Stir thoroughly, cover with a lid and microwave HIGH for 15 minutes stirring twice during cooking. Leave to rest for 5 minutes or more. Serve on a bed of rice.

Spicy Potato and Cauliflower

Serves 8

INGREDIENTS	Imperial	Metric	American
Onions, sliced	*2 medium*	*2 medium*	*2 medium*
Garlic	*2 cloves*	*2 cloves*	*2 cloves*
Vegetable oil	*1 tbsp*	*1 tbsp*	*1 tbsp*
New potatoes	*8 oz*	*225 g*	*2 cups*
Cauliflower	*1 medium*	*1 medium*	*1 medium*
Cumin seeds	*1 tsp*	*1 tsp*	*1 tsp*
Coriander seeds	*1/2 tsp*	*1/2 tsp*	*1/2 tsp*
Mustard seeds	*1 tsp*	*1 tsp*	*1 tsp*
Nutmeg	*1 tsp*	*1 tsp*	*1 tsp*
Curry powder	*1 tsp*	*1 tsp*	*1 tsp*
Water or white wine	*2 tbsp*	*2 tbsp*	*2 tbsp*
Salt			
Pepper			

GARNISH
Fresh parsley, coriander or mint

1. Slice the onions and garlic and place with vegetable oil in a glass bowl. Microwave HIGH for 3 minutes.

2. Wash the new potatoes and slice, leaving the skins on. Clean the cauliflower and remove the stalks. Cut into florets. Combine with the onions in a casserole and add the seasonings. Stir well. Cover with a lid or plate, leaving a gap to allow steam to escape. Microwave HIGH for 15 minutes, stirring twice during cooking.

3. Serve garnished with freshly chopped parsley, coriander or mint.

Aubergine and Potato Moussaka

Serves 8

INGREDIENTS	Imperial	Metric	American
Aubergines	2 medium	2 medium	2 medium
Sea salt	2 tsp	2 tsp	2 tsp
Butter	2 oz	50 g	2 oz
Onions	2 medium	2 medium	2 medium
Garlic	2 cloves	2 cloves	2 cloves
Potatoes	2 large	2 large	2 large
Tin of tomatoes	14 oz	400 g	14 oz
Basil	1 tsp	1 tsp	1 tsp
Sea salt	1 tsp	1 tsp	1 tsp
Plain yoghurt	1 pt	600 ml	2½ cups
Eggs	2	2	2
Sea salt			
Freshly ground pepper			
Paprika			
GARNISH			
Watercress salad			

1. Cut the aubergines into slices and sprinkle with salt. Leave for 15 minutes. Turn over and repeat on the other side. Scrape off salt and pat dry with kitchen paper. This process brings out the bitter minerals in the aubergines.

2. Melt the butter by microwaving on HIGH for 1 minute. Slice the onions, garlic and potatoes. Put in a glass bowl. Pour over the butter and stir. Cover with a lid or plate, leaving a gap to allow steam to escape. Microwave HIGH for 7 minutes.

3. Combine the tinned tomatoes, tomato purée, basil and salt in a food processor and process for 2 minutes.

4. In a casserole, make layers of tomato sauce, aubergine and potatoes until all the ingredients are used.

Combine the yoghurt, eggs, salt and pepper and pour over the vegetables. Sprinkle with paprika. Bake on HI-SPEED for 15 minutes at 250°C. Or microwave HIGH for 5 minutes, then grill to brown if liked. Garnish with watercress.

Stuffed Cabbage Leaves

Serves 6

INGREDIENTS	Imperial	Metric	American
Cabbage leaves	6	6	6
Onion, chopped	1 medium	1 medium	1 medium
Celery, chopped	1 stick	1 stick	1 stick
Carrot, grated	1 medium	1 medium	1 medium
Vegetable oil	1 tbsp	1 tbsp	1 tbsp
Cooked rice	6 tbsp	6 tbsp	6 tbsp
Vegetable stock	4 tbsp	4 tbsp	4tbsp
Parsley, chopped	2 tbsp	2 tbsp	2 tbsp
Cumin seeds	1 tsp	1 tsp	1 tsp
Salt	1 tsp	1 tsp	1 tsp
Pepper	1 tsp	1 tsp	1 tsp
Parmesan cheese	2 tbsp	2 tbsp	2 tbsp
Butter	2 oz	50 g	2 oz

1. Separate the leaves from a cabbage or spring greens and wash thoroughly. Place in a glass bowl suitable for microwave and cover with a lid or plate, leaving a gap to allow steam to escape. Microwave HIGH for 5 minutes. Remove and cool. The leaves should now be quite pliable.

2. Place the chopped onion, celery and carrot in a glass bowl, add the oil and microwave HIGH for 3 minutes. Combine with the cooked rice, vegetable stock, herbs and seasonings. Flatten the cabbage leaves and carefully place about 2 tablespoonfuls of the stuffing in the centre of each. Make a tidy parcel of each leaf and place in a casserole. Sprinkle with Parmesan cheese and place a knob of butter on each leaf. Microwave HIGH for 8 minutes.

Cheese, Egg and Potato Pie

Serves 8

INGREDIENTS	Imperial	Metric	American
Wholemeal flour	*6 oz*	*150 g*	*6 oz*
Pinch of salt			
Butter	*2 oz*	*50 g*	*2 oz*
Salt	*½ tsp*	*½ tsp*	*½ tsp*
Iced water	*3 tbsp*	*3 tbsp*	*3 tbsp*
or			
Frozen pastry	*8 oz*	*225 g*	*8 oz*
Potato	*2 medium*	*2 medium*	*2 medium*
Hard boiled egg, chopped	*2*	*2*	*2*
Cheddar cheese, grated	*4 oz*	*100 g*	*4 oz*
Double cream	*4 – 5 oz*	*130 g*	*1 cup*
Salt	*1 tsp*	*1 tsp*	*1 tsp*
Pepper	*1 tsp*	*1 tsp*	*1 tsp*
Fresh chives	*1 tsp*	*1 tsp*	*1 tsp*

1. Make the pastry by sieving the flour and salt into a bowl. Rub in the butter until it resembles fine breadcrumbs. Mix with the water. Rest for 30 minutes. If using frozen pastry, allow to defrost well ahead of time. Roll the pastry out and line a pie dish.

2. Peel and cube the potatoes and place on the pastry case. Combine the chopped hard boiled eggs, grated cheese and double cream with the salt and pepper and fresh chives. Pour on top of the potatoes in the pastry case. Place pastry lid on top and decorate. Cook HI-SPEED at 250°C for 30 minutes. Or microwave HIGH for 10 minutes.

Deep Wholemeal Pizza

Serves 6

INGREDIENTS	Imperial	Metric	American
PIZZA DOUGH			
Lukewarm water	*5 tbsp*	*5 tbsp*	*5 tbsp*
Dried yeast	*1/2 oz*	*15 g*	*1/2 oz*
Caster sugar	*1/2 tsp*	*1/2 tsp*	*1/2 tsp*
Plain white flour	*4 oz*	*100 g*	*1 cup*
Wholewheat flour	*4 oz*	*100 g*	*1 cup*
Sea salt	*1 tsp*	*1 tsp*	*1 tsp*
Butter or margarine	*2 oz*	*50 g*	*1/4 cup*
Egg	*1 medium*	*1 medium*	*1 medium*
FILLING			
Tin of tomatoes	*14 oz*	*400 g*	*14 oz*
Onions	*2 medium*	*2 medium*	*2 medium*
Garlic	*2 cloves*	*2 cloves*	*2 cloves*
Mushrooms	*4 oz*	*100 g*	*1 cup*
Grûyére cheese	*4 oz*	*100 g*	*1 cup*
Basil	*1 tsp*	*1 tsp*	*1 tsp*
Sea salt			
Freshly ground black pepper			

1. Combine the warm water, dried yeast and sugar and leave to activate for 10 minutes.

2. Sieve the flour into a bowl with the salt and rub in the butter. Add the yeast liquid and the beaten egg and work into a stiff dough.

3. Knead well on a lightly floured surface until smooth. Place in a bowl, cover with cling film and leave in a warm place until doubled in size.

4. Prepare the filling by placing the tin of tomatoes in a food processor and process for 2 minutes. Slice the onions, garlic and mushrooms quite finely.

5. Return to the dough. Knock back and knead again for a few minutes. Divide into 6 pieces and make 6 individual pizzas by piling tomato, onions, mushrooms and cheese on each. Season to taste. Rest for 20 minutes then bake in the microwave on HI-SPEED for 20 minutes at 250°C. Or microwave HIGH for 7 minutes.

Vegetarian Cornish Pastry

Serves 8

INGREDIENTS	Imperial	Metric	American
Wholemeal flour	*6 oz*	*150 g*	*6 oz*
Butter	*2 oz*	*50 g*	*2 oz*
or Frozen Pastry	*8 oz*	*225 g*	*8 oz*
FILLING			
Onion, chopped	*2 medium*	*2 medium*	*2 medium*
Carrot, chopped	*2 medium*	*2 medium*	*2 medium*
Potato, chopped	*2 medium*	*2 medium*	*2 medium*
Turnip, chopped	*2 medium*	*2 medium*	*2 medium*
Frozen peas	*2 tbsp*	*2 tbsp*	*2 tbsp*
Fresh parsley or			
coriander	*2 tbsp*	*2 tbsp*	*2 tbsp*
Salt	*1 tsp*	*1 tsp*	*1 tsp*
Pepper	*1 tsp*	*1 tsp*	*1 tsp*
Mustard seeds	*1 tsp*	*1 tsp*	*1 tsp*
Cumin seeds	*1 tsp*	*1 tsp*	*1 tsp*
Egg, beaten	*1 tsp*	*1 tsp*	*1 tsp*
GARNISH			
Watercress			

1. Make the pastry by rubbing the butter into the flour until it looks like fine breadcrumbs. Combine with iced cold water and allow to rest. Roll out and cut about 8 circles from the pastry with a saucer or something similar. Spread out.

2. Chop and dice the onion, carrot, potato and turnip and combine together in a bowl with the frozen peas and the seasonings. Place 2 tablespoons of the filling in the centre of each circle of pastry. Brush around the outside with egg, bringing the sides up and joining together along the top. Make a zigzag pattern and brush with egg. Repeat 8 times. Place on a plate and cook HI-SPEED for 25 minutes or until brown at 250°C. Or microwave HIGH for 9 minutes.

Almond, Carrot and Potato Loaf

Serves 8

INGREDIENTS	Imperial	Metric	American
Butter	*2 oz*	*50 g*	*¼ cup*
Onion	*1 medium*	*1 medium*	*1 medium*
Garlic	*2 cloves*	*2 cloves*	*2 cloves*
Fresh wholewheat breadcrumbs	*10 oz*	*275 g*	*3 cups*
Carrots, grated	*8 oz*	*225 g*	*2½ cups*
Flaked almonds	*4 oz*	*100 g*	*1 cup*
Potato, grated	*1 small*	*1 small*	*1 small*
Eggs	*2 large*	*2 large*	*2 large*
Lemon juice	*1 medium*	*1 medium*	*1 medium*
Nutmeg	*½ tsp*	*½ tsp*	*½ tsp*
Paprika	*½ tsp*	*½ tsp*	*½ tsp*
Sea salt	*1 tsp*	*1 tsp*	*1 tsp*
Freshly ground black pepper			

GARNISH
Tomato and onion salad

1. Place the butter in a glass bowl and microwave HIGH for 1 minute. Add the onion and garlic and microwave HIGH for 3 minutes. Rest.

2. In a large bowl combine the breadcrumbs, grated carrot, flaked almonds and grated potato. Add the onion and garlic mixture. Beat the eggs and add these with the lemon juice and seasonings.

3. Place in a greased loaf dish 18 × 12 × 8 cm/7½ × 5 × 3½ in and bake at HI-SPEED for 20 minutes at 250°C. Or microwave HIGH for 7 minutes. Test by inserting a knife. If it comes out clean it is cooked. If not, cook for a further 3 minutes.

4. Serve garnished with a tomato and onion salad.

Pepper, Courgette and Onion Quiche

Serves 8

INGREDIENTS	Imperial	Metric	American
PASTRY			
Plain flour	*8 oz*	*225 g*	*2 cups*
Sea salt	*½ tsp*	*½ tsp*	*½ tsp*
Butter or margarine	*2 oz*	*50 g*	*¼ cup*
Vegetable lard	*2 oz*	*50 g*	*¼ cup*
Iced water	*4 fl oz*	*120 ml*	*½ cup*
FILLING			
Butter or margarine	*2 oz*	*50 g*	*¼ cup*
Onions	*2 medium*	*2 medium*	*2 medium*
Garlic	*2 cloves*	*2 cloves*	*2 cloves*
Red pepper	*1 large*	*1 large*	*1 large*
Courgettes	*2 medium*	*2 medium*	*2 medium*
Eggs	*4 large*	*4 large*	*4 large*
Plain yoghurt or cream	*4 tbsp*	*4 tbsp*	*4 tbsp*
Milk	*4 fl oz*	*125 ml*	*½ cup*
Cheddar cheese	*4 oz*	*100 g*	*1 cup*
Sea salt	*1 tsp*	*1 tsp*	*1 tsp*
Paprika	*1 tsp*	*1 tsp*	*1 tsp*
Freshly ground black pepper			

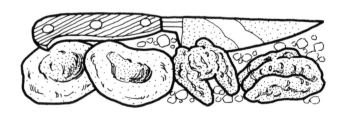

1. Make the pastry by sifting the flour and salt into a bowl. Cut in the butter and lard. Add sufficient water to make a soft dough. Form into a ball and leave to rest in the fridge for half an hour.

2. Place the butter in a glass bowl and microwave HIGH for 1 minute. Chop the onion, garlic and red pepper. Slice the courgettes. Place in the bowl and microwave HIGH for 5 minutes. Alternatively, this can be stir-fried on the hob.

3. Roll out the pastry and line a flan dish. Place cooled vegetables on the pastry base leaving liquid behind. Combine eggs, yoghurt, milk, cheese and salt and pour into flan. Sprinkle with paprika and pepper. Bake at HI-SPEED on 250°C for 20 minutes. Or microwave HIGH for 7 minutes.

Nut Roast

Serves 8

INGREDIENTS	Imperial	Metric	American
Butter	*2 oz*	*50 g*	*¼ cup*
Onions	*2 medium*	*2 medium*	*2 medium*
Garlic	*3 cloves*	*3 cloves*	*3 cloves*
Mixed nuts, ground	*8 oz*	*225 g*	*2 cups*
Fresh wholewheat breadcrumbs	*10 oz*	*275 g*	*3 cups*
Marmite	*1 tsp*	*1 tsp*	*1 tsp*
Water	*4 fl oz*	*120 ml*	*½ cup*
Sea salt	*1 tsp*	*1 tsp*	*1 tsp*
Nutmeg	*½ tsp*	*½ tsp*	*½ tsp*
Freshly chopped parsley	*2 tbsp*	*2 tbsp*	*2 tbsp*
Freshly ground black pepper			

GARNISH
Watercress salad

1. Melt the butter in a glass bowl by microwaving on HIGH for 1 minute. Add the sliced onion and garlic. Stir together and microwave HIGH for 3 minutes.

2. In a large bowl combine the nuts and the freshly grated wholewheat breadcrumbs and add the onion and garlic mixture. Combine the marmite with the water and add to the mixture along with the seasonings. The mixture should be firm but not sticky. Add more water if necessary.

3. Place in a greased loaf dish 18 × 12 × 8/7½ × 5 × 3 × ½ inches and bake on HI-SPEED for 20 minutes at 250°C. Or microwave HIGH for 7 minutes. Allow to cool slightly before serving. Serve with a watercress salad.

Baked Potato Surprise

Serves 6

INGREDIENTS	Imperial	Metric	American
Potatoes	6	6	6
Vegetable oil	*1 tsp*	*1 tsp*	*1 tsp*
Soured cream	*5 fl oz*	*150 ml*	*5 fl oz*
Cottage cheese	*4 oz*	*100 g*	*1 cup*
Fresh chives	*1 tbsp*	*1 tbsp*	*1 tbsp*
Sea salt			
Fresh ground black pepper			
Cheddar cheese	*4 oz*	*100 g*	*1 cup*
Cashew nuts	*4 oz*	*100 g*	*1 cup*
GARNISH			
Watercress salad			

1. Scrub the potatoes clean and prick with a fork. Place a few drops of oil on the palm of your hand and rub each potato with it. Place on a plate or flat dish and microwave HIGH for 10 minutes. Test to see if cooked and microwave for a further 2 minutes if necessary. Remove and cool a little.

2. Combine the soured cream, cottage cheese and chives with the salt and pepper. Cut the potatoes in half but not completely. Remove some of the potato, not all, and mix with the soured cream mixture. Put this mixture back into the potato and carefully push together again leaving a crack about an inch wide. Place on the plate and cover each potato with grated cheese and push cashew nuts into the cracks. Microwave HIGH for 5 minutes.

3. Serve with a watercress salad.

Vegetable Curry

Serves 6

INGREDIENTS	Imperial	Metric	American
Vegetable oil	2 tbsp	2 tbsp	2 tbsp
Cardamon seeds	6	6	6
Whole cloves	6	6	6
Cumin seeds	1 tsp	1 tsp	1 tsp
Onions	2 medium	2 medium	2 medium
Garlic	2 cloves	2 cloves	2 cloves
Celery	1 stick	1 stick	1 stick
Leeks	1 medium	1 medium	1 medium
Red pepper	1 medium	1 medium	1 medium
Courgettes	2 medium	2 medium	2 medium
Cauliflower	1 small	1 small	1 small
Potato	1 medium	1 medium	1 medium
Carrots	2 medium	2 medium	2 medium
Curry powder	1 tbsp	1 tbsp	1 tbsp
Chinese 5 spice	1 tsp	1 tsp	1 tsp
Vegetable stock	1 pt	600 ml	3 cups
Cornflour	1 tbsp	1 tbsp	1 tbsp
Sea salt			
Freshly ground black pepper			
GARNISH			
Rice			

1. Place the oil, cardamon seeds, cloves, cumin seeds, chopped onion, garlic and celery in a large glass bowl and microwave HIGH for 3 minutes.

2. In the meantime, prepare the remaining vegetables. Deseed and defibre the red pepper and chop. Slice the courgettes and cut the cauliflower into florets. Peel and cube the potato and slice the carrots.

3. Place all the vegetables in a bowl and sprinkle the curry powder and Chinese 5 spice over them. Mix a little of the cornflour into the stock to make a paste then combine the two and pour over the vegetables.

4. Cover with a lid or plate, leaving a gap to allow steam to escape. Microwave **HIGH** for 15 minutes stirring twice during the cooking process. Test that the vegetables are not overdone.

5. Serve on a bed of rice.

Stuffed Marrow

Serves 6

INGREDIENTS	Imperial	Metric	American
Marrow	*1 medium*	*1 medium*	*1 medium*
Vegetable oil			
Onion	*1 medium*	*1 medium*	*1 medium*
Garlic	*2 cloves*	*2 cloves*	*2 cloves*
Mushrooms	*4 oz*	*100 g*	*1 cup*
Cooked rice	*4 oz*	*100 g*	*1 cup*
Vegetable stock	*2 tbsp*	*2 tbsp*	*2 tbsp*
Nutmeg	*1 tsp*	*1 tsp*	*1 tsp*
Sea salt	*1 tsp*	*1 tsp*	*1 tsp*
Freshly ground black pepper			
GARNISH			
Parmesan Cheese			

1. Peel the marrow and cut in half but not completely and remove the seeds. Place open in a shallow casserole with a few tablespoons of water on the bottom.

2. In a glass bowl, place the oil, chopped onion, garlic and mushrooms and microwave HIGH for 3 minutes. Remove and combine with the cooked rice, stock and seasonings.

3. Pile the stuffing into the marrow and push together but not completely. Microwave HIGH for 15 minutes or until the marrow is tender.

4. Allow to rest for 2 minutes and sprinkle with parmesan cheese. Serve with hot wholemeal bread.

4 PASTA, GRAINS & PULSES

Pasta and rice can be cooked in a microwave oven but no time is really saved in the cooking process. The advantage is that it will not stick or burn as there is no direct heat.

The microwave is ideal for reheating pasta or rice dishes. They can be cooked from frozen on a HIGH setting or MEDIUM if there is a delicate sauce which would curdle.

These days, in many areas, it is possible to buy fresh pasta which is preferable and ideal for the microwave. The majority of the following recipes are using fresh pasta which has been boiled in a little salt and a little vegetable oil to stop the pasta sticking together. It is always important not to overcook pasta. Really fresh pasta should only need 3 or 4 minutes if it has dried out a little. If dried pasta is used, allow 12 minutes and allow 5 minutes standing time.

After cooking pasta in a microwave oven it should be allowed to rest to complete the cooking. Turn over occasionally. This is an ideal time to prepare or reheat a sauce but be sure to keep it in a warm place.

Similarly, pulses take a long time to cook in a microwave and in some cases, are not very successful. Red kidney beans and broad beans in particular tend to get toughened skins. All pulses should be soaked, preferably overnight. Even lentils benefit by a short soak. In many cases a tinned variety of kidney beans, chick peas or broad beans for instance, is often preferable or use beans which have been cooked on a conventional hob. They are, however, an essential part of a vegetarian diet.

Fresh Green Tagliatelle and Pesto Sauce

Serves 6

INGREDIENTS	Imperial	Metric	American
Boiling water			
Fresh green tagliatelle	8 oz	225 g	3 cups
Sea salt	2 tsp	2 tsp	2 tsp
Vegetable oil	1 tbsp	1 tbsp	1 tbsp
SAUCE			
Fresh basil or coriander	2 oz	50 g	2 oz
Parmesan cheese	2 oz	50 g	2 oz
Pine nuts or walnuts	2 oz	50 g	2 oz
Olive oil	2 tbsp	2 tbsp	2 tbsp
Sea salt	1 tsp	1 tsp	1 tsp
Freshly ground black pepper			
GARNISH			
Parmesan Cheese	2 oz	50 g	2 oz

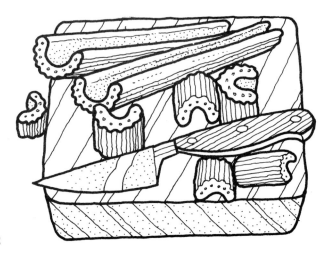

1. Boil a kettle and three-quarters fill an ovenproof glass bowl with boiling water. Shake the tagliatelle apart and add to the water with salt and vegetable oil. Cover with a lid or plate, leaving a gap to allow steam to escape. Microwave HIGH for 3 minutes, a minute longer if the fresh pasta has dried out a little.

2. Drain and leave to rest in a warm place, turning occasionally.

3. Pick over the basil or coriander and remove the stalks. Place in food processor with all the other ingredients and process for 2 minutes. If every thick add a little more oil. Place in a bowl and microwave MEDIUM for 3 minutes. Combine with the tagliatelle and microwave HIGH for 1 minute if necessary. Serve immediately with parmesan cheese and fresh French bread.

Tagliatelle with Spinach

Serves 6

INGREDIENTS	Imperial	Metric	American
Boiling water			
Fresh tagliatelle			
* or spaghetti*	*8 oz*	*225 g*	*3 cups*
Sea salt	*2 tsp*	*2 tsp*	*2 tsp*
Vegetable oil	*1 tbsp*	*1 tbsp*	*1 tbsp*
Butter	*2 oz*	*50 g*	*2 oz*
SAUCE			
Spinach	*8 oz*	*225 g*	*1/2 lb*
Ricotta cheese	*4 oz*	*650 g*	*1 cup*
Egg yolks	*2*	*2*	*2*
Single cream	*2 tbsp*	*2 tbsp*	*2 tbsp*
Nutmeg	*1/2 tsp*	*1/2 tsp*	*1/2 tsp*
Salt			
Pepper			

1. Place the boiling water in an ovenproof glass bowl or casserole. Shake out the fresh tagliatelle or spaghetti and place in the water along with the salt and vegetable oil. Cover with a lid or plate, leaving a gap to allow steam to escape. Microwave HIGH for 3 minutes, a minute longer if the pasta has dried out a little. Drain and leave to rest. Add the butter, turning occasionally.

2. In the meantime, clean the spinach and remove the stalks. Place in a glass bowl, cover with a lid or plate, leaving a gap to allow steam to escape. Microwave HIGH for 8 minutes. Drain if necessary. Place in a food processor with the ricotta cheese, egg yolks and cream. Process for 1 minute. Add seasoning.

3. Combine with the noodles and serve immediately.

Canneloni with Courgettes

Serves 8

INGREDIENTS	Imperial	Metric	American
Canneloni	*8 ¹/₂ oz*	*250 g*	*8 ¹/₂ oz*
Boiling water			
Onions, chopped	*2 medium*	*2 medium*	*2 medium*
Garlic, chopped	*2 cloves*	*2 cloves*	*2 cloves*
Courgettes, sliced	*6 medium*	*6 medium*	*6 medium*
Vegetable oil			
Salt	*1 tsp*	*1 tsp*	*1 tsp*
Pepper	*1 tsp*	*1 tsp*	*1 tsp*
Cottage cheese	*4 oz*	*115 g*	*4 oz*
Nutmeg	*¹/₂ tsp*	*¹/₂ tsp*	*¹/₂ tsp*
Butter	*2 oz*	*50 g*	*2 oz*
Flour	*1 tbsp*	*1 tbsp*	*1 tbsp*
Milk	*1 pt*	*600 ml*	*1 pt*
Salt	*¹/₂ tsp*	*¹/₂ tsp*	*¹/₂ tsp*
Cheddar cheese, grated	*2 oz*	*50 g*	*2 oz*
Flaked almonds	*2 oz*	*50 g*	*2 oz*

GARNISH
Freshly chopped coriander or parsley

1. Place the canneloni in a large casserole and three-quarters fill with boiling water. Microwave HIGH for 15 minutes. Rest in the water for 5 minutes then drain and cool.

2. Place the chopped onions and garlic in a glass bowl and microwave HIGH for 3 minutes. Remove and place carefully in a food processor with the cottage cheese and seasoning. Process for 1 minute. Stuff this mixture into the canneloni and place in the casserole.

3. Make the cheese sauce by melting the butter. Microwave HIGH for 30 seconds. Add the flour and stir thoroughly. Add the milk. Microwave HIGH for 2 minutes. Add the cheese and seasoning and microwave HIGH for a further 2 minutes. Stir thoroughly then pour over the canneloni.

4. Sprinkle with flaked almonds and microwave HIGH for 10 minutes. Rest for 5 minutes before serving. Serve garnished with freshly chopped coriander or parsley.

Macaroni Cheese

Serves 6

INGREDIENTS	Imperial	Metric	American
Boiling water			
Wholewheat macaroni	*8 oz*	*225 g*	*2 cups*
Sea salt	*1 tsp*	*1 tsp*	*1 tsp*
Vegetable oil	*1 tbsp*	*1 tbsp*	*1 tbsp*
Butter	*2 oz*	*50 g*	*1/4 cup*
Flour	*2 oz*	*50 g*	*1/4 cup*
Milk	*1 pt*	*600 ml*	*3 cups*
Cheddar cheese	*8 oz*	*225 g*	*2 cups*
Sea salt			
Freshly ground black pepper			
Tomatoes	*2 medium*	*2 medium*	*2 medium*
Sunflower seeds	*2 tbsp*	*2 tbsp*	*2 tbsp*
GARNISH			
Green salad			

1. Boil the water in a kettle and pour over the macaroni which is in a bowl with the salt and vegetable oil. Place in the oven and microwave HIGH for 12 minutes. Rest for 2 minutes then drain. Place in casserole.

2. In a large glass jug melt the butter microwaving HIGH for 1 minute. Add the flour and combine thoroughly. Add the milk and microwave HIGH for 3 minutes stirring twice during the cooking time. On the last stir add half the cheese, reserving the rest for the top. Season to taste.

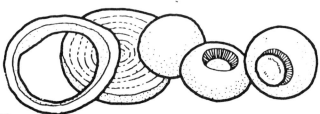

3. Pour the cheese sauce over the macaroni. Slice the tomatoes and place on the top with the remaining Cheddar cheese and the sunflower seeds.

4. Place in the oven and HI-SPEED for 10–12 minutes until the top is browned. Allow to rest for 2 minutes. Or microwave HIGH for 3-4 minutes, then grill to brown if liked. Serve with salad.

Wild Rice with Vegetables

Serves 8

INGREDIENTS	Imperial	Metric	American
Wild rice, soaked	4 oz	100 g	1 cup
Brown rice, soaked	4 oz	100 g	1 cup
Boiling water	1 ½ pt	900 ml	5 cups
Olive oil	1 tbsp	1 tbsp	1 tbsp
Sea salt	1 tsp	1 tsp	1 tsp
Onion	1 medium	1 medium	1 medium
Olive oil	1 tsp	1 tsp	1 tsp
Garlic, crushed	2 cloves	2 cloves	2 cloves
Red pepper	1 medium	1 medium	1 medium
Mushrooms	4 medium	4 medium	4 medium
Courgettes	2 medium	2 medium	2 medium
Water	2 tbsp	2 tbsp	2 tbsp
Salt			
Pepper			
GARNISH			
Fresh herbs			

1. Soak the wild and brown rice separately, preferably overnight. Rinse through by washing the soaking rice under running water. Place in a large bowl with the boiling water, olive oil and sea salt. Stir well, cover with a lid or plate, leaving a gap to allow steam to escape and microwave HIGH for 30 minutes. Stir twice during the cooking. Rest for 5 minutes.

2. In the meantime, prepare the vegetables. Slice the onion and place with the oil and garlic in a glass bowl. Microwave HIGH for 3 minutes. Add the chopped peppers, mushrooms and courgettes and sprinkle on the water and seasoning. Cover as before and microwave HIGH for 10 minutes. Combine the rice and the vegetables and garnish with fresh herbs.

Italian Risotto

Serves 8

INGREDIENTS	Imperial	Metric	American
Long grain rice, soaked	8 oz	225 g	8 oz
Onions, chopped	2 medium	2 medium	2 medium
Garlic, chopped	2 cloves	2 cloves	2 cloves
Vegetable oil	1 tbsp	1 tbsp	1 tbsp
Celery, chopped	1 stick	1 stick	1 stick
Mushrooms, sliced	2 oz	50 g	2 oz
Tin of tomatoes	14 oz	400 g	14 oz
Tomato purée	2 tbsp	2 tbsp	2 tbsp
Water	2 tbsp	2 tbsp	2 tbsp
Salt	1 tsp	1 tsp	1 tsp
Pepper	1 tsp	1 tsp	1 tsp
Basil	1 tsp	1 tsp	1 tsp
Pine nuts	2 tbsp	2 tbsp	2 tbsp
Parmesan cheese	2 tbsp	2 tbsp	2 tbsp

GARNISH
Freshly chopped parsley.

1. Soak the long grain rice and place in a casserole. Place the chopped onion and garlic in a bowl suitable for microwave and sprinkle on the oil. Microwave HIGH for 3 minutes. Add the celery and mushrooms. Microwave HIGH for a further 3 minutes.

2. Process the tin of tomatoes with the tomato puree, water and seasonings in a food processor for 1 minute. Mix with the vegetables and pour onto the rice. Stir thoroughly. Sprinkle the pinenuts and Parmesan cheese on the top. Microwave HIGH for 20 minutes. Rest for a further 5 minutes. Serve garnished with parsley.

Fresh Fuselli with Fresh Vegetables

Serves 6

INGREDIENTS	Imperial	Metric	American
Boiling water			
Fresh fuselli	8 oz	225 g	3 cups
Sea salt	2 tsp	2 tsp	2 tsp
Vegetable oil	1 tbsp	1 tbsp	1 tbsp
SAUCE			
Onion	1 medium	1 medium	1 medium
Garlic	2 cloves	2 cloves	2 cloves
Celery	1 stick	1 stick	1 stick
Red pepper	1 medium	1 medium	1 medium
Vegetable oil	2 tbsp	2 tbsp	2 tbsp
Sea salt	1 tsp	1 tsp	1 tsp
Freshly ground black pepper			
GARNISH			
Cheddar cheese, grated	2 oz	50 g	1 cup

1. Boil a kettle and three-quarters fill an ovenproof glass bowl with boiling water. Add the fuselli, salt and vegetable oil. Cover with a lid or plate, leaving a gap to allow steam to escape. Microwave HIGH for 5 minutes. Drain and leave to rest in a warm place.

2. Chop the onion, garlic, celery and red pepper. Place in a glass bowl, sprinkle with the oil, salt and pepper. Cover with a lid or plate, leaving a gap to allow steam to escape. Microwave HIGH for 5 minutes.

3. Combine the vegetables with the fuselli and sprinkle with the Cheddar cheese. Microwave HIGH for 2 minutes. Serve with hot French bread.

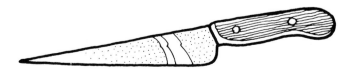

Fresh Pasta Shells and Tomato Sauce

Serves 6

INGREDIENTS	Imperial	Metric	American
Boiling water			
Fresh pasta shells	*8 oz*	*225 g*	*3 cups*
Sea salt	*2 tsp*	*2 tsp*	*2 tsp*
Vegetable oil	*1 tbsp*	*1 tbsp*	*1 tbsp*
SAUCE			
Butter or margarine	*2 oz*	*50 g*	*2 oz*
Onions	*2 medium*	*2 medium*	*2 medium*
Garlic	*2 cloves*	*2 cloves*	*2 cloves*
Tin of tomatoes	*14 oz*	*400 g*	*14 oz*
Tomato purée	*2 tbsp*	*2 tbsp*	*2 tbsp*
Basil	*1 tsp*	*1 tsp*	*1 tsp*
Sea Salt	*1 tsp*	*1 tsp*	*1 tsp*
Freshly ground black pepper			
GARNISH			
Parmesan cheese			

1. Boil a kettle and three-quarters fill an ovenproof glass bowl with boiling water. Add the fresh pasta shells, salt and oil and microwave HIGH for 5 minutes or until tender. Drain and place in a warm place to rest.

2. Place the butter in a bowl and microwave HIGH for 1 minute. Add the sliced onion and garlic and microwave HIGH for 3 minutes.

3. In a food processor, combine the tinned tomatoes, tomato purée, basil, salt and pepper and process for 2 minutes.

4. Add to the onion mixture and microwave HIGH for 3 minutes. Combine the pasta shells with the tomato sauce and garnish with parmesan cheese.

Green Lentil and Mushroom Layer

Serves 8

INGREDIENTS	Imperial	Metric	American
Green lentils, soaked	8 oz	225 g	8 oz
Onions, chopped	2 medium	2 medium	2 medium
Garlic	2 cloves	2 cloves	2 cloves
Vegetable oil	1 tbsp	1 tbsp	1 tbsp
Celery, chopped	1 stick	1 stick	1 stick
Flat mushrooms, sliced	8 oz	225 g	8 oz
Salt and pepper			
Cheddar cheese	4 oz	100 g	4 oz
Butter	2 oz	50 g	2 oz
Flour	1 tbsp	1 tbsp	1 tbsp
Salt and pepper			
Parmesan cheese	2 oz	50 g	2 oz
Nutmeg	$1/2$ tsp	$1/2$ tsp	$1/2$ tsp

1. Soak the lentils overnight and pick out any black ones. Place in boiling water and microwave HIGH for 20 minutes. Drain away excess water and place to one side to cool.

2. Slice the onions and garlic. Sprinkle on the oil and microwave HIGH for 3 minutes. Add the chopped celery, sliced mushrooms and salt and pepper. Microwave HIGH for 3 minutes.

3. Make layers of lentils and mushrooms ending with a mushroom layer. Make the cheese sauce by grating the cheese. Place the butter in a glass bowl and microwave HIGH for 30 seconds. Add the flour and stir thoroughly. Add the milk and microwave for 2 minutes. Stir thoroughly and add the cheese. Microwave HIGH for 2 minutes. Stir thoroughly then pour over the lentil and mushroom layers. Sprinkle the Parmesan cheese on the top and HI-SPEED for 25 minutes. Or microwave HIGH for 9 minutes, then grill to brown if liked. Allow to rest before serving.

Spicy Spaghetti with Mushrooms

Serves 6

INGREDIENTS	Imperial	Metric	American
Boiling water			
Fresh spaghetti	*8 oz*	*225 g*	*3 cups*
Sea salt	*1 tsp*	*1 tsp*	*1 tsp*
Vegetable oil	*1 tbsp*	*1 tbsp*	*1 tbsp*
SAUCE			
Butter or margarine	*2 oz*	*50 g*	*2 oz*
Flour	*1 oz*	*25 g*	*1 oz*
Mushrooms	*4 oz*	*100 g*	*4 oz*
Paprika	*½ tsp*	*½ tsp*	*½ tsp*
Nutmeg	*½ tsp*	*½ tsp*	*½ tsp*
Single cream	*2 tbsp*	*2 tbsp*	*2 tbsp*
GARNISH			
Parmesan cheese	*2 oz*	*50 g*	*2 oz*

1. Boil a kettle of water and three-quarters fill an ovenproof glass bowl with boiling water. Separate the fresh spaghetti by shaking at apart and add to the water with the salt and vegetable oil. Microwave HIGH for 3 minutes or until tender. Drain and keep warm.

2. Place the butter in a glass bowl and microwave HIGH for 1 minute. Add the flour and mix well. Wash and slice the mushrooms. Add with the spices to the butter and flour mixture. Stir well. Cover with a lid or plate, leaving a gap to allow steam to escape. Microwave HIGH for 7 minutes, stirring twice during cooking. Add the cream and stir well. Combine with the spaghetti and serve garnished with Parmesan cheese.

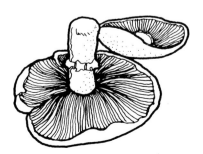

Spanish Rice with Nuts and Raisins

Serves 6

INGREDIENTS	Imperial	Metric	American
Butter or margarine	2 oz	50 g	2 oz
Onion	1 medium	1 medium	1 medium
Garlic	2 cloves	2 cloves	2 cloves
Red pepper	1 medium	1 medium	1 medium
Celery	1 stick	1 stick	1 stick
Hot green chilli	1 small	1 small	1 small
Mushrooms	4 oz	100 g	2 cups
Long grain rice (soaked)	7 oz	200 g	2^1/$_2$ cups
Boiling vegetable stock	14 fl oz	400 ml	5 cups
Paprika	^{1}/$_2$ tsp	^{1}/$_2$ tsp	^{1}/$_2$ tsp
Sea salt	1^1/$_2$ tsp	1^1/$_2$ tsp	1^1/$_2$ tsp
Freshly ground black pepper			
GARNISH			
Mixed nuts	2 oz	50 g	^{1}/$_2$ cup
Raisins	2 oz	50 g	^{1}/$_2$ cup

1. Place the butter in a large casserole and microwave HIGH for 1 minute. Chop the onion, garlic, red pepper, celery, hot green chilli and the mushrooms and add to the butter. Stir well together and cover with a lid or plate, leaving a gap to allow steam to escape. Microwave HIGH for 5 minutes.

2. Wash the rice and soak briefly. Add with the boiling vegetable stock and seasoning to the casserole. Cover with a lid or plate, leaving a gap to allow steam to escape. Microwave HIGH for 12 minutes or until the rice is tender. Stir twice during cooking process.

3. Remove from the oven and allow to rest for 5 minutes. Add the chopped nuts and the raisins. Serve with a green salad.

Vegetarian Kedgeree

Serves 6

INGREDIENTS	Imperial	Metric	American
Smoked tofu	8 oz	225 g	2 cups
Boiling water	1 pt	600 ml	2½ cups
Butter	1 oz	25 g	2 tbsp
Onion, sliced	1 medium	1 medium	1 medium
Garlic, chopped	1 clove	1 clove	1 clove
Red pepper, chopped	1 medium	1 medium	1 medium
Green pepper chopped	1 medium	1 medium	1 medium
Long grain rice	6 oz	150 g	¾ cup
Turmeric	1 tsp	1 tsp	1 tsp
Chinese 5 spice	1 tsp	1 tsp	1 tsp
Sea salt			
Freshly ground black pepper			
Hard-boiled eggs	3	3	3
Parmesan cheese	1 tbsp	1 tbsp	1 tbsp

1. Chop the tofu and boil the water. Place the butter in a bowl and microwave HIGH for 1 minute. Add the vegetables and microwave for a further 2 minutes. Add all the other ingredients and cook for 15 minutes, stirring twice. Add more liquid if necessary.

2. Add the hard-boiled eggs and sprinkle with Parmesan cheese. Microwave HI-SPEED for 5 minutes and serve. Or microwave HIGH for 2 minutes.

Wild Rice and Peas with Ginger

Serves 6

INGREDIENTS	Imperial	Metric	American
Butter or margarine	2 oz	50 g	2 oz
Onion	1 medium	1 medium	1 medium
Garlic	3 cloves	3 cloves	3 cloves
Hot chilli	1 medium	1 medium	1 medium
Cumin seeds	1/2 tsp	1/2 tsp	1/2 tsp
Long grain rice (soaked)	7 oz	200 g	2 1/2 cups
Wild rice (soaked)	2 oz	50 g	1/2 cup
Boiling vegetable stock	14 fl oz	400 ml	6 cups
Fresh ginger root (optional)	1 in	2.5 cm	1 in
Sea salt	2 tsp	2 tsp	2 tsp
Nutmeg	1/2 tsp	1/2 tsp	1/2 tsp
Chinese 5 spice	1/2 tsp	1/2 tsp	1/2 tsp
Paprika	1/2 tsp	1/2 tsp	1/2 tsp
Freshly ground black pepper			
Fresh garden peas (Frozen peas may be used instead)	4 oz	100 g	1 cup

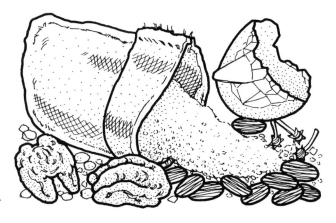

1. Place the butter in a large casserole and microwave HIGH for 1 minute. Chop the onion, garlic and hot chilli and add with the cumin seeds to the butter and microwave HIGH for 5 minutes.

2. Add the soaked long grain and wild rice along with the boiling vegetable stock, chopped ginger root and seasonings. Cover with a lid or plate, leaving a gap to allow steam to escape. Microwave HIGH for 8 minutes.

3. Remove from the oven. Add the garden peas and stir well. Cover as before. Microwave HIGH for a further 8 minutes or until the rice is tender. Allow to stand for 5 minutes to complete cooking.

Barley with Vegetables and Cheese

Serves 6

INGREDIENTS	Imperial	Metric	American
Pearl barley	*7 oz*	*200 g*	*2½ cups*
Butter or margarine	*2 oz*	*50 g*	*2 oz*
Onion	*1 medium*	*1 medium*	*1 medium*
Red pepper	*1 medium*	*1 medium*	*1 medium*
Courgette	*1 medium*	*1 medium*	*1 medium*
Leeks	*1 medium*	*1 medium*	*1 medium*
Mushrooms	*2 oz*	*50 g*	*2 oz*
Boiling vegetable stock	*¼ pt*	*150 ml*	*⅔ cup*
Sea salt	*1 tsp*	*1 tsp*	*1 tsp*
Nutmeg	*½ tsp*	*½ tsp*	*½ tsp*
Ground cumin	*½ tsp*	*½ tsp*	*½ tsp*
Freshly ground black pepper			
GARNISH			
Cheddar cheese	*2 oz*	*50 g*	*2 oz*
Fresh chopped parsley	*2 tbsp*	*2 tbsp*	*2 tbsp*

1. Soak the pearl barley in warm water for at least 2 hours. Place the butter in a large casserole and microwave HIGH for 1 minute. Chop the onion, red pepper, courgette, leeks and mushrooms and add to the butter. Mix well and sprinkle with a little water. Microwave HIGH for 5 minutes.

2. Drain the pearl barley and add to the casserole. Add the boiling vegetable stock and the seasonings. Cover with a lid or plate, leaving a gap to allow steam to escape. Microwave HIGH for 12 minutes or until the barley is cooked al dente. It should not be overcooked.

3. Garnish with grated cheese and freshly chopped parsley.

Three-Bean Casserole

Serves 8

INGREDIENTS	Imperial	Metric	American
Red kidney beans	¹/₂ lb	225 g	1 cup
Black-eyed aduki beans	¹/₂ lb	225 g	1 cup
Butter beans	¹/₂ lb	225 g	1 cup
Onions	2 medium	2 medium	2 medium
Garlic	2 cloves	2 cloves	2 cloves
Vegetable oil	2 tbsp	2 tbsp	2 tbsp
Tinned tomatoes	14 oz	400 g	14 oz
Tomato purée	2 tbsp	2 tbsp	2 tbsp
Ginger root	1 in	2.5 cm	1 in
Nutmeg	1 tsp	1 tsp	1 tsp
Cumin seed	1 tsp	1 tsp	1 tsp
Sea salt	1 tsp	1 tsp	1 tsp
Freshly ground black pepper			

1. Soak the beans and cook separately on the hob. The black-eyed beans need 20 minutes, the kidney beans need 40 minutes and the butter beans 35 minutes, all in plenty of boiling water. (Tinned beans can be used for this recipe.) Drain and cool.

2. Chop and slice the onion and the garlic and place in a glass bowl. Pour on the oil and microwave HIGH for 3 minutes.

3. Add all the remaining ingredients, chopping the tomatoes, and mix thoroughly. Place in a casserole. Microwave HIGH for 10 minutes stirring twice during the cooking process.
   Leave to stand for 5 minutes before serving.

Buckwheat and Walnut Casserole

Serves 6

INGREDIENTS	Imperial	Metric	American
Buckwheat	*7 oz*	*200 g*	*2¹/₂ cups*
Butter and margarine	*2 oz*	*50 g*	*2 oz*
Onions	*2 medium*	*2 medium*	*2 medium*
Garlic	*2 cloves*	*2 cloves*	*2 cloves*
Red or green pepper	*1 medium*	*1 medium*	*1 medium*
Potatoes	*2 large*	*2 large*	*2 large*
Boiling vegetable stock	*1 pt*	*600 ml*	*1 pt*
Walnuts	*2 oz*	*50 g*	*2 oz*
Sea salt	*1 tsp*	*1 tsp*	*1 tsp*
Paprika	*¹/₂ tsp*	*¹/₂ tsp*	*¹/₂ tsp*
Cumin	*¹/₂ tsp*	*¹/₂ tsp*	*¹/₂ tsp*
Nutmeg	*¹/₂ tsp*	*¹/₂ tsp*	*¹/₂ tsp*
Freshly ground black pepper			

GARNISH
Chopped parsley

1. Soak the buckwheat for at least 2 hours in warm water.

2. Place the butter in a large casserole and microwave HIGH for 1 minute. Add a chopped onion, garlic and pepper along with the cubed potato. Microwave HIGH for 5 minutes.

3. Drain the buckwheat and add to the vegetables along with the boiling vegetable stock and seasonings. Cover with a lid or plate, leaving a gap to allow steam to escape. Microwave HIGH for 12 minutes stirring twice during cooking.

4. Allow to rest for 5 minutes before serving garnished with chopped parsley.

Split Pea and Fennel Bake with Honey

Serves 6

INGREDIENTS	Imperial	Metric	American
Green split peas	1 lb	500 g	4 cups
Vegetable oil	2 tbsp	2 tbsp	2 tbsp
Onions	2 medium	2 medium	2 medium
Garlic	2 cloves	2 cloves	2 cloves
Fennel	1 bulb	1 bulb	1 bulb
Honey	2 tbsp	2 tbsp	2 tbsp
Boiling vegetable stock	1 pt	600 ml	1 pt
Sea salt	1 tsp	1 tsp	1 tsp
Nutmeg	1/2 tsp	1/2 tsp	1/2 tsp
Ground cumin	1/2 tsp	1/2 tsp	1/2 tsp
Mint	1/2 tsp	1/2 tsp	1/2 tsp

1. Soak the split peas overnight and pick out any bad or discoloured ones.

2. Place the vegetable oil in a large casserole and add the chopped onion, garlic and fennel. Microwave HIGH for 5 minutes.

3. Drain the split peas and add the honey, boiling vegetable stock and seasonings. Cover with a lid or plate, leaving a gap to allow steam to escape. Microwave HIGH for 20 minutes stirring twice during the cooking process. Uncover.

4. Allow to rest and complete the cooking for 5 to 10 minutes.
   Serve with a freshly baked potato garnished with soured cream and freshly chopped mint and chives.

Lentil Provençal

Serves 6

INGREDIENTS	Imperial	Metric	American
Red lentils	7 oz	200 g	2½ cups
Vegetable oil	2 tbsp	2 tbsp	2 tbsp
Onion	1 medium	1 medium	1 medium
Garlic	3 cloves	3 cloves	3 cloves
Hot green chilli	1 medium	1 medium	1 medium
Courgette	1 medium	1 medium	1 medium
Tomatoes	3 medium	3 medium	3 medium
Boiling vegetable stock	1 pt	600 ml	1 pt
Chilli powder	½ tsp	½ tsp	½ tsp
Ground cumin	½ tsp	½ tsp	½ tsp
Ground nutmeg	½ tsp	½ tsp	½ tsp
Ground turmeric	½ tsp	½ tsp	½ tsp
Sea salt	1 tsp	1 tsp	1 tsp
Freshly ground black pepper			

GARNISH
Freshly chopped
   parsley or coriander

1. Pick over the lentils and soak for at least 2 hours. Drain.

2. In a large casserole place the oil, chopped onion, garlic and chilli. Microwave HIGH for 3 minutes. Add the red lentils and stir well together. Microwave HIGH for 3 minutes.

3. Chop the courgette and tomatoes quite finely and add to the lentils with the boiling vegetable stock. Cover with a lid or plate, leaving a gap to allow steam to escape. Microwave HIGH for 20 minutes, stirring twice during the cooking.

4. Allow to rest for 5 minutes to complete cooking.
   Serve garnished with freshly chopped parsley and hot fresh wholemeal bread.

Lentil, Carrot and Celery Stew

Serves 6 ~ 3

INGREDIENTS

		Imperial	Metric	American
Onions	*1*	2 medium	2 medium	2 medium
Garlic	*1*	2 cloves	2 cloves	2 cloves
Cumin seeds	*½ tsp*	1 tsp	1 tsp	1 tsp
Vegetable oil	*1 Tables*	2 tbsp	2 tbsp	2 tbsp
Root ginger	*¼*	½ in	1 cm	½ in
Red pepper	*small*	1 medium	1 medium	1 medium
Celery	*1*	2 sticks	2 sticks	2 sticks
Carrots	*1½*	2 medium	2 medium	2 medium
Red lentils	*3½*	7 oz	175 g	7 oz
Vegetable stock	*¼*	1 pt	600 ml	2½ cups
Nutmeg	*½*	1 tsp	1 tsp	1 tsp
Sea salt	*½*	1 tsp	1 tsp	1 tsp
Freshly ground black pepper	*✓*			
GARNISH				
Sunflower seeds	*2 o 2.4 oz*		100 g	4 oz

1. Slice the onions and garlic and place with the cumin seeds in a glass bowl with the vegetable oil. Microwave HIGH for 3 minutes.

2. Prepare the remaining vegetables. Chop the ginger root really finely. Slice the red pepper and celery and carrot. Soak and thoroughly pick over the red lentils. Place these vegetables with the stock and seasonings in the glass bowl and microwave HIGH for 15 minutes stirring twice during the cooking process.

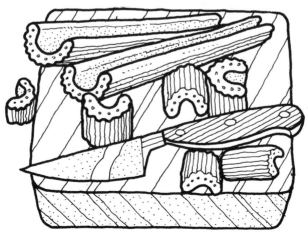

Chick Pea and Tomato Casserole

Serves 6-8

INGREDIENTS	Imperial	Metric	American
Chick peas	*1 lb*	*500 g*	*3 cups*
or tinned chick peas	*2 × 15 oz*	*2 × 430 g*	*2 × 15 oz*
Butter or margarine	*2 oz*	*50 g*	*2 oz*
Onions	*2 medium*	*2 medium*	*2 medium*
Garlic	*2 cloves*	*2 cloves*	*2 cloves*
Tin of tomatoes	*14 oz*	*400g*	*14 oz*
Tomato purée	*2 tbsp*	*2 tbsp*	*2 tbsp*
Sea salt	*1 tsp*	*1 tsp*	*1 tsp*
Paprika	*1/2 tsp*	*1/2 tsp*	*1/2 tsp*
Cumin	*1/2 tsp*	*1/2 tsp*	*1/2 tsp*
Ground coriander	*1/2 tsp*	*1/2 tsp*	*1/2 tsp*
Freshly ground			
black pepper			

GARNISH
Freshly chopped
coriander leaves

1. Soak the dried chick peas overnight. Pick out discoloured peas. Drain. Cover with boiling water and microwave HIGH for 30 minutes. Alternatively, drain the tinned chick peas.

2. In a large casserole, place the butter and microwave HIGH for 1 minute. Add the chopped onion and garlic and microwave HIGH for 3 minutes.

3. Place the tinned tomatoes, tomato purée and seasonings in a food processor and process for 2 minutes. Taste and correct for seasoning. Add to the onion mixture and mix well.

4. Add the drained chick peas and mix all the ingredients together well. Microwave HIGH for 10 minutes.

5. Allow to rest for 5 minutes to complete the cooking.
   Garnish with freshly chopped coriander.

5 DESSERTS

Gooseberry Fool

Serves 8

INGREDIENTS	Imperial	Metric	American
Gooseberries	1 lb	500 g	3 cups
Soft brown sugar	1 tbsp	1 tbsp	1 tbsp
Lemon juice	1 tsp	1 tsp	1 tsp
Butter	1 oz	25 g	1 oz
Flour	2 tbsp	2 tbsp	2 tbsp
Milk	8 fl oz	225 ml	2 cups
Caster sugar	2 tbsp	2 tbsp	2 tbsp
Double cream	5 oz	140 g	1 cup

1. Top and tail the gooseberries and wash thoroughly. Place in a bowl and sprinkle with the sugar and lemon juice. Microwave HIGH for 5 minutes. Cool.

2. Place the butter in a glass measuring jug and microwave HIGH for 20 seconds. Stir in the flour and mix thoroughly. Add a little milk and stir well. Add remaining milk and microwave HIGH for 1 minute. Remove. Stir well and add the sugar. Microwave HIGH for 1 minute. Remove and stir. Return to microwave on HIGH for a further minute.

3. Place the gooseberries and the custard in a food processor and process for 2 minutes. In the meantime, whip the double cream. When the mixture is cool combine together. Serve really cold in individual ramekins or a large glass bowl.

Pineapple Upside-Down Cake

Serves 6

INGREDIENTS	Imperial	Metric	American
Pineapple slices	5	5	5
Butter	*1 oz*	*25 g*	*1 tbsp*
Golden syrup	*2 tbsp*	*2 tbsp*	*2 tbsp*
Butter	*6 oz*	*175 g*	*½ cup*
Soft brown sugar	*6 oz*	*175 g*	*½ cup*
Eggs	*3 medium*	*3 medium*	*3 medium*
Plain flour	*6 oz*	*175 g*	*1 cup*
Baking powder	*1 tbsp*	*1 tbsp*	*1 tbsp*
Vanilla essence	*1 tsp*	*1 tsp*	*1 tsp*
Greek yoghurt	*5 oz*	*140 g*	*1 cup*

1. Lay the pineapple slices on some kitchen paper. Fresh or tinned can be used. In a casserole big enough to take 5 slices of pineapple, place the ounce of butter along with the golden syrup. Microwave HIGH for 20 seconds. Place the pineapple in the mixture and grease the sides of the dish.

2. Cream the butter and sugar together until light and fluffy. Beat the eggs together and add to the mixture with a little of the sieved flour. Add remaining flour and baking powder and mix lightly together. Add the vanilla essence and pour the mixture on top of the pineapple.

3. Microwave HIGH for 12 minutes. Leave to cool in the dish for 5 minutes then turn out and serve with yoghurt.

Black Cherries in Wine with Lemon Cream

Serves 6

INGREDIENTS	Imperial	Metric	American
Black cherries	1 lb	500 g	3 cups
Red or white wine	3 tbsp	3 tbsp	3 tbsp
Caster sugar (Optional)	1 tsp	1 tsp	1 tsp
Double cream or yoghurt	5 oz	140 g	1 cup
Zest of lemon	1	1	1

1. Remove the stalks from the cherries and wash thoroughly. Place in a heatproof bowl and sprinkle the wine and sugar over the cherries. Microwave HIGH for 3 minutes.

2. Whip the double cream until soft peaks are formed then spread over the cherries. (Greek yoghurt is an excellent alternative for those watching their weight.) Sprinkle with lemon zest and microwave HIGH for 1 minute.

Dried Fruit Compote

Serves 8

INGREDIENTS	Imperial	Metric	American
Prunes	*8 oz*	*250 g*	*1 cup*
Apricots	*8 oz*	*250 g*	*1 cup*
Dried apples	*4 oz*	*125 g*	*½ cup*
Dried pears	*4 oz*	*125 g*	*½ cup*
Sultanas	*1 tbsp*	*1 tbsp*	*1 tbsp*
Walnuts	*1 tbsp*	*1 tbsp*	*1 tbsp*
Clear honey	*1 tbsp*	*1 tbsp*	*1 tbsp*
White wine or water	*4 fl oz*	*4 fl oz*	*1 cup*

1. Soak the prunes either overnight in cold water or for half an hour in boiling water. Remove the stones if there are any. Combine the prunes, apricots, apple rings, pears and sultanas in a bowl suitable for microwaves. Chop the walnuts and combine with the honey. Sprinkle over the dried fruit. Add the liquid, white wine or water and microwave HIGH for 10 minutes. Cool.

2. Serve with muesli for a healthy breakfast or with cream as a dessert.

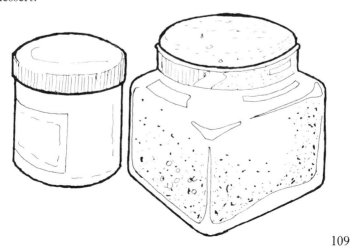

Summer Pudding

Serves 8

INGREDIENTS	Imperial	Metric	American
Strawberries	*½ lb*	*250 g*	*2 cups*
Raspberries	*1 ½ lb*	*750 g*	*3 cups*
Black cherries	*¼ lb*	*125 g*	*1 cup*
Redcurrants	*¼ lb*	*125 g*	*1 cup*
Blackcurrants	*¼ lb*	*125 g*	*1 cup*
Caster sugar	*2 tbsp*	*2 tbsp*	*2 tbsp*
Water	*3 tbsp*	*3 tbsp*	*3 tbsp*
White sliced loaf	*1 large*	*1 large*	*1 large*
Whipped cream	*5 oz*	*140 g*	*1 cup*

1. Remove the hulls from the strawberries and raspberries and wash only if necessary. Remove stalks and stones from the cherries and put with the strawberries and raspberries in a glass bowl suitable for microwave. Remove the stems and stalks from the red and blackcurrants and mix with the other fruit. Sprinkle over the sugar and water.

2. Microwave HIGH for 3 minutes. Remove. Stir well and microwave HIGH for another minute. Do not overcook. Remove the crusts from the bread and line a bowl, overlapping the bread as you go. Spoon in a layer of fruit then cover with a few slices of bread. Add another layer of fruit and so on until all that remains is a little juice. Reserve this juice. The final layer should be bread.

3. Place in the fridge with a weighted place on the top overnight. Turn out and pour remaining juice over the top. Serve with cream.

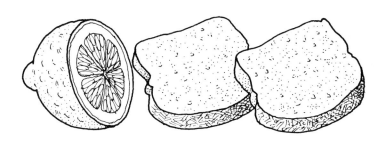

Apricot and Almond Flambé

Serves 6

INGREDIENTS	Imperial	Metric	American
Fresh apricots	1 lb	500 g	3 cups
Apricot jam	2 tbsp	2 tbsp	2 tbsp
Apricot brandy	2 tbsp	2 tbsp	2 tbsp
Flaked almonds	2 tbsp	2 tbsp	2 tbsp
Double cream	5 oz	140 g	1 cup
Whisky	1 tbsp	1 tbsp	1 tbsp

1. Clean the apricots and remove the stones. Place in a glass bowl suitable for microwave. Spread the apricot jam over the fruit and splash on the brandy. (White wine would make a good alternative.) Microwave HIGH for 5 minutes. Cool.

2. Spread the flaked almonds on a huge plate and HI-SPEED for 6 minutes or until golden brown. Alternatively, toast under the grill. Whip the cream until soft peaks appear and place on the apricot mixture. Sprinkle over the almonds.

3. Just before serving, heat a spoon under the hot tap. Pour the whisky into the spoon and ignite with a match. Pour ignited over the apricots and serve at once.

Baked Apples with Almonds and Dates

Serves 4

INGREDIENTS	Imperial	Metric	American
Cooking apples	4 medium	4 medium	4 medium
Fresh dates	4	4	4
Flaked almonds	1 tbsp	1 tbsp	1 tbsp
Soft brown sugar	1 tbsp	1 tbsp	1 tbsp
Water	1 tbsp	1 tbsp	1 tbsp
Lemon juice	1 tbsp	1 tbsp	1 tbsp
Caster sugar	1 tbsp	1 tbsp	1 tbsp
Greek yoghurt	5 oz	140 g	1 cup

1. Wash and de-core the apples but do not peel. Cut a line around the centre of the apple and place them in a casserole suitable for a microwave. Combine the chopped fresh dates with the flaked almonds and the soft brown sugar and place in the core of each apple.

2. Mix the water, lemon juice and caster sugar together and sprinkle a little over each apple. Cover the casserole with a lid or plate, leaving a gap to allow steam to escape. Microwave HIGH for 8 minutes. Remove from the oven and allow to rest still covered for at least 5 minutes. Serve with a spoonful of Greek yoghurt or any plain yoghurt.

Spicy Conference Pears

Serves 8

INGREDIENTS	Imperial	Metric	American
Conference pears	8	8	8
Whole cloves	16	16	16
Maple syrup	2 tbsp	2 tbsp	2 tbsp
Red wine	½ bottle	½ bottle	½ bottle
Nutmeg	1 tsp	1 tsp	1 tsp
Single cream or yoghurt	5 oz	140 g	1 cup

1. Peel the pears leaving the stalk intact. Press 2 whole cloves into each pear or more if liked. Place the pears in a casserole suitable for microwave and dribble maple syrup over each pear. Pour on half a bottle of ordinary red table wine. (White will do but does not produce such a good colour.) Sprinkle with nutmeg and cover with a lid or plate, leaving a gap to allow steam to escape.

2. Microwave HIGH for 10 minutes. Remove from oven. Check to see how tender the pears are. Turn and baste well with the wine. Cover again and microwave HIGH for a further 5 minutes. Allow to rest before serving. May be served hot or cold with or without cream or yoghurt.

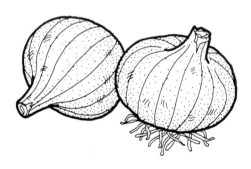

Apple and Walnut Crumble

Serves 8

INGREDIENTS	Imperial	Metric	American
Cooking apples	4 medium	4 medium	4 medium
Butter	1 oz	25 g	1 tbsp
Caster sugar	2 oz	50 g	2 tbsp
Water	2 tbsp	2 tbsp	2 tbsp
Butter	2 oz	50 g	2 tbsp
Flour	4 oz	100 g	1 cup
Rolled oats	2 tbsp	2 tbsp	2 tbsp
Soft brown sugar	2 tbsp	2 tbsp	2 tbsp
Chopped walnuts	2 tbsp	2 tbsp	2 tbsp
Nutmeg	1 tsp	1 tsp	1 tsp
Fresh cream or yoghurt			

1. Peel, core and slice the apples and place in a casserole suitable for microwave. Dot with the ounce of butter and sprinkle with the sugar and water. Microwave HIGH for 4 minutes. Remove. Stir well and mash up a little.

2. Make the crumble by rubbing the butter into the flour and adding the rolled oats, sugar, walnuts and nutmeg. Spoon on top of the apple and press down lightly. Microwave at HI-SPEED 250°C for 15 minutes. Or microwave HIGH for 5 minutes, then grill to brown if liked. Serve hot or cold with fresh cream or plain yoghurt.

Spotted Dick with Custard

Serves 6

INGREDIENTS	Imperial	Metric	American
Butter	*4 oz*	*100 g*	*½ cup*
Soft brown sugar	*4 oz*	*100 g*	*½ cup*
Eggs	*3*	*3*	*3.*
Self-raising flour	*6 oz*	*150 g*	*1 cup*
Raisins	*1 tbsp*	*1 tbsp*	*1 tbsp*
Sultanas	*1 tbsp*	*1 tbsp*	*1 tbsp*
Currants	*1 tbsp*	*1 tbsp*	*1 tbsp*
Milk	*2 tbsp*	*2 tbsp*	*2 tbsp*
CUSTARD			
Custard powder	*1 tbsp*	*1 tbsp*	*1 tbsp*
Caster sugar	*1 tbsp*	*1 tbsp*	*1 tbsp*
Milk	*½ pt*	*8 fl oz*	*8 fl oz*

1. Cream the butter and the sugar together until light and fluffy. Beat the eggs and add to the creamed mixture with a little of the sieved flour. Add remaining flour and the fruit and mix together briefly with the milk.

2. Place in a greased Pyrex casserole and HI-SPEED at 250°C for 15 minutes. Or microwave HIGH for 5 minutes. Test with a knife so that it comes out clean. Rest for 5 minutes before serving.

3. To make the custard, combine the custard powder and the sugar. Add the milk and mix thoroughly. Microwave HIGH for 3 minutes, stirring twice during the cooking.

Creme Brûleé

Serves 8

INGREDIENTS	Imperial	Metric	American
Milk	1 pt	600 ml	1 pt
Eggs	4	4	4
Vanilla caster sugar	5 tbsp	5 tbsp	5 tbsp
Double cream	5 oz	140 g	1 cup
Greek yoghurt	5 oz	140 g	1 cup
Soft brown sugar	4 tbsp	4 tbsp	4 tbsp

1. Place the milk in a glass bowl and microwave HIGH for 3 minutes being careful not to boil the milk. Beat the eggs and caster sugar together. Sieve this mixture into the milk. Beat the yoghurt and cream together and add to the mixture. Cover with a lid or plate, leaving a gap to allow steam to escape.

2. Place the bowl in a larger bowl containing boiling water (Bain-Marie) and microwave LOW for 20 minutes. Allow to cool in the fridge. Sprinkle the sugar on the top of the pudding and grill until the sugar has caramelised. Allow to cool then serve.

Bread and Butter Pudding

Serves 8

INGREDIENTS	Imperial	Metric	American
Bread and butter slices	8	8	8
Sultanas	2 oz	50 g	½ cup
Caster sugar	2 tbsp	2 tbsp	2 tbsp
Milk	1 pt	600 ml	1 pt
Strong black coffee	2 tbsp	2 tbsp	2 tbsp
Eggs	3	3	3
Nutmeg	1 tsp	1 tsp	1 tsp

1. Grease a flameproof casserole suitable for microwave and line with four slices of the bread and butter. Sprinkle the sultanas and caster sugar over the bread.

2. Place the milk and the coffee in a glass bowl and microwave HIGH for 2 minutes. Beat the eggs together then pour the milk over them, stirring all the time. Pour this mixture over the bread then place the remaining bread and butter slices, butter side up, on top. Press down into the mixture and leave to soak for 5 minutes.

3. Place in the oven and cook HI-SPEED for 15 minutes. Or microwave LOW for 12 minutes, then grill to brown if liked.

Creme Caramel

Serves 4

INGREDIENTS	Imperial	Metric	American
CARAMEL			
Caster sugar	*2 level tbsp*	*2 level tbsp*	*2 level tbsp*
Water	*4 tbsp*	*4 tbsp*	*4 tbsp*
CUSTARD			
Milk	*12 fl oz*	*350 ml*	*12 fl oz*
Caster sugar	*1 tbsp*	*1 tbsp*	*1 tbsp*
Eggs	*2*	*2*	*2*

1. Mix the sugar and water together and place in Pyrex casserole. Microwave HIGH for 2 minutes. Turn the dish and microwave HIGH for a further 2 minutes until caramelised. Remove and cool.

2. Place the milk and sugar in a glass bowl or jug and microwave HIGH for 2 minutes. Stir well. Beat the eggs then pour the hot milk mixture on to the eggs. Stir well. Strain through a sieve onto the caramel. Cover with a lid or plate, leaving a gap to allow steam to escape.

3. Microwave LOW for 8 minutes, turning the dish a quarter turn every 2 minutes. Remove from the oven and leave to stand covered to continue cooking.

French Apple Tart

Serves 6

INGREDIENTS	Imperial	Metric	American
PASTRY			
Plain flour	*8 oz*	*225 g*	*1 cup*
Salt	*Pinch*	*Pinch*	*Pinch*
Butter	*2 oz*	*50 g*	*¼ cup*
Vegetable lard	*2 oz*	*50 g*	*¼ cup*
Iced water	*3 tbsp*	*3 tbsp*	*3 tbsp*
FILLING			
Golden Delicious			
apples	*4 medium*	*4 medium*	*4 medium*
Apricot jam	*2 tbsp*	*2 tbsp*	*2 tbsp*
Water	*2 tbsp*	*2 tbsp*	*2 tbsp*

1. Make the pastry by sieving the flour and salt together and rubbing or cutting in the fat. Combine quickly with iced water and leave to rest in the fridge for 30 minutes.
Roll out on a floured board and line a 9 in (23 cm) flan dish.

2. Cut the apples in quarters. Remove the core but do not peel. Cut in thin slices and place in layers in the pastry, overlapping each other thus creating an interesting pattern.

3. Combine the jam and water in a glass measuring jug and microwave HIGH for 2 minutes. Stir and pour over the apples. Cook HI-SPEED at 250°C for 15 minutes. Or microwave HIGH for 5 minutes.

Lemon Cheesecake

Serves 6

INGREDIENTS	Imperial	Metric	American
Butter	*2 oz*	*50 g*	*4 tbsp*
Digestive biscuit crumbs	*4 oz*	*100 g*	*1 cup*
Cream cheese	*6 oz*	*175 g*	*1 cup*
Eggs	*2*	*2*	*2*
Caster sugar	*3 oz*	*75 g*	*⅓ cup*
Lemon, juice and rind	*1*	*1*	*1*
Double cream	*5 oz*	*140 g*	*1 cup*
GARNISH			
Whipped Cream			

1. Place the butter in a glass measuring jug and microwave HIGH for 1 minute. Combine with the digestive biscuit crumbs and press into a 9 in (23 cm) flan dish.

2. In a food processor or a bowl, combine the cream cheese, eggs and caster sugar and process for 1 minute. Take zest to taste from the lemon and put to one side. Add the juice to the mixture and the double cream. Process for 1 minute. Pour on top of the biscuit mixture and sprinkle the zest on top. Spoon the zest in a swirling movement.

3. Microwave MEDIUM for 14 minutes. Remove and allow to cool before serving. Serve with whipped cream. Serves 6.

Apple and Apricot Compôte

Serves 4

INGREDIENTS	Imperial	Metric	American
Eating apples	*2*	*2*	*2*
Brown sugar	*1 ½ oz*	*40 g*	*3 tbsp*
Canned apricot halves	*1 lb*	*450 g*	*1 lb*
Chopped walnuts	*2 oz*	*50 g*	*½ cup*
Ground cinnamon	*¼ tsp*	*¼ tsp*	*¼ tsp*
Pinch of ground nutmeg			
Pinch of ground cloves			

1. Peel and core the apples and cut into thin slices. Put into a casserole and sprinkle with sugar. Cover and microwave HIGH for 3 minutes.

2. Drain the apricots and stir the fruit into the apples. Add 4 tablespoons syrup from the can. Stir in the nuts and spices. Microwave HIGH uncovered for 4 minutes. Serve warm with cream. Canned peach slices, pears or pineapple may be used instead of apricots.

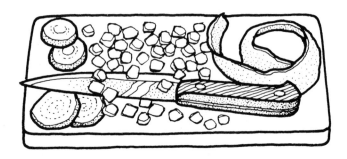

Baked Apples

Serves 4

INGREDIENTS	Imperial	Metric	American
Cooking apples	4 large	4 large	4 large
Maple syrup	¼ pint	150 ml	⅔ cup
Butter	1 oz	25 g	2 tbsp

1. Core the apples without peeling them, and score round the skin with a sharp knife. Put the apples in a shallow dish and pour syrup over them. Put a piece of butter in the centre of each apple. Cover with a lid or plate, leaving a gap to allow steam to escape. Microwave HIGH for 8 minutes. Serve hot with cream or custard.

Brown Sugar Apples
Prepare the apples in the same way, but substitute 2 oz/50 g/4 tablespoons dark soft brown sugar and 4 tablespoons water for the maple syrup.

Spiced Pears

Serves 4

INGREDIENTS	Imperial	Metric	American
Pears	4	4	4
Red wine	1/2 pt.	300 ml	1 1/4 cups
Water	1/2 pt	300 ml	1 1/4 cups
Brown sugar	2 oz	50 g	4 tbsp
Cinnamon stick	1 x 2 ins	1 x 5 cm	1 x 2 ins
Cloves	4	4	4
Pinch of ground nutmeg			
Piece of lemon peel			
Lemon juice	1/2 tsp	1/2 tsp	1/2 tsp
Flaked almonds	2 tbsp	2 tbsp	2 tbsp

1. The pears should be ripe but firm, and even-sized. Peel them carefully and leave the fruit whole with the stalks on. Put the wine, water, sugar, spices, lemon peel and juice into a pie dish and microwave HIGH for 5 minutes. Stand the pears in the liquid with stalks uppermost. Microwave HIGH for 5 minutes.

2. Leave to stand for 5 minutes, spooning the liquid over the pears a few times. Remove the cinnamon stick, cloves and lemon peel. Sprinkle each pear with almonds and serve with cream.

Caramel Oranges

Serves 4

INGREDIENTS	Imperial	Metric	American
Oranges	*4*	*4*	*4*
Caster sugar	*6 oz*	*150 g*	*¾ cup*
Water	*7 tbsp*	*100 ml*	*7 tbsp*
Orange liqueur	*1 tbsp*	*15 ml*	*1 tbsp*

1. Peel the oranges carefully, making sure that all the white pith is removed. Cut across in slices and arrange in a serving dish. Sprinkle with the orange liqueur. Put the sugar and water into a basin and stir well.

2. Cook in the microwave oven for 12 minutes HIGH until dark golden. Pour over the oranges and chill before serving.

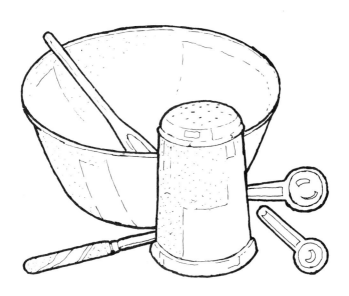

Index

Pasta Shells and Tomato Sauce, Fresh 88
Pea and Nutmeg Soup, Green 13
Pears, Spiced 124
Pepper, Courgette and Onion Quiche 70
Peppers, Stuffed Red 32
Pineapple Upside-Down Cake 106
Pizza, Deep Wholemeal 66
Potato and Cauliflower, Spicy 61
Potato Surprise, Baked 73
Pumpkin Soup, Spicy 26

Rataouille 37
Rice and Peas with Ginger, Wild 94
Rice with Nuts and Raisins 92
Rice with Vegetables, Wild 84
Risotto, Italian 85

Spaghetti with Mushrooms, Spicy 90

Spinach Florentine 38
Spinach, Parsnip and Carrot Terrine 48
Spinach Ricotta Layer 54
Split Pea and Fennel Bake with Honey 100
Spotted Dick with Custard 116
Summer Pudding 110

Tagliatelle and Pesto Sauce, Fresh Green 78
Tagliatelle with Spinach 80
Tofu with Bean Sprouts 33
Tomato and Orange Soup 18
Tomatoes, Stuffed 30

Vegetable Kebab, Mixed 45
Vegetable Soup, Chinese 14
Vegetable Soup, Slimming 29
Vegetable Stir-Fry, Chinese 53
Vegetarian Hot Pot 52
Vine Leaves, Stuffed 49

Watercress Soup 28